"As a war correspondent in London during the worst days of the blitz," writes Quentin Reynolds, "I saw what one great human being—namely, Winston Churchill—could do to hold together a nation literally on the verge of being annihilated."

Here is the story of this great man's "finest hour" during the troubled years of World War II, as well as countless other highlights of his long, many-faceted career. From rebellious schoolboy to daring young soldier, author, politician, historian and statesman, the reader follows Winston Churchill through more than a half-century of stormy, courageous and colorful leadership in peace and war.

Winston Churchill

Winston Churchill

by Quentin Reynolds

illustrated
with photographs

Random House / New York

Grateful acknowledgment is made to:
Cassell & Company, Limited, and Houghton Mifflin Company for permission to use on pages 112, 124, 145 and 151 quotations from THE SECOND WORLD WAR by Winston S. Churchill (Volume 1. The Gathering Storm; Volume 2. Their Finest Hour; Volume 4. The Hinge of Fate; Volume 6. Triumph and Tragedy). Published 1948, 1949, 1951 and 1954 by Cassell & Company, Limited, London. Copyright 1948, 1949, 1950 and 1953 by Houghton Mifflin Company, Boston.

Doubleday and Company, Inc., for permission to use on pages 139 and 140 information and a quotation from THE TURN OF THE TIDE by Arthur Bryant, copyright © 1957 by Arthur Bryant.

Farrar, Straus & Company for permission to use on pages 133 and 134 information and a quotation from ASSIGNMENT: CHURCHILL by Walter Henry Thompson.

Odhams Press Limited and Charles Scribner's Sons for permission to use on pages xiii, 16, 26, 27, 37, 38, 39, 43 and 44 information and quotations from MY EARLY LIFE by Winston S. Churchill.

Odhams Press Limited and Charles Scribner's Sons for permission to use on page 91 a quotation from THE WORLD CRISIS by Winston S. Churchill.

Photograph credits: The Bettmann Archive, Inc., pages 36, 43, 65; British Information Services, 5, 75, 143, 147, 150 bottom; Brown Brothers, 48, 80, 83; Culver Pictures, 3, 11; Daily Herald of London, 15; Imperial War Museum, 88; P.I.P. Photos by Radio Times Hulton Picture Library, xii, 24, 103, 106; Pix, viii, 55, 98, 118, 129, 150 top; P. A. Reuter, 68; Marc Riboud from Magnum, ii; United Press International, 128, 133, 153, 172; United States Army, 158, 160; Wide World Photos, 109, 113, 115, 125, 163. Cover photograph: United Press International. Endpapers: British Information Services (front); Marc Riboud from Magnum (back).

CIP data may be found at the end of the book.

Designed by Jane Byers

Library of Congress catalog card number: 63–7831

5th Edition

Contents

PART THREE
THE FINEST HOUR

MAPS

Prologue

The spring of 1940 was a perilous time for Great Britain.

The powerful armies of Nazi Germany had overrun Poland, Norway, Denmark, The Netherlands and Belgium. France was surely doomed. Only Great Britain remained a stumbling block to German plans for western European conquest. But how long could she hold out alone?

In the British House of Commons, a stoop-shouldered, freckle-faced, elder statesman rose from his seat to deliver an unforgettable answer to the question:

"We shall go on to the end. We shall fight in France, we shall fight in the seas and oceans, we shall fight with growing confidence and growing strength in the air; we shall defend our Island, whatever the cost may be. . . ."

The elder statesman was Winston Churchill. Under his magnificent leadership, the English people responded with such vigor, courage and determination that, in the end, Britain withstood the Nazi war machine.

This is Winston Churchill's story.

PART ONE

THE DAYS OF REBELLION
AND ADVENTURE

*"I was happy as a child with my toys
in my nursery. I have been
happier every year since I became
a man. But this interlude of
school makes a sombre grey patch
upon the chart of my journey."*

The Boy Winston

On an August day in 1873, the seventh Duke of Marlborough received a distressing letter from his younger son, Lord Randolph Churchill. His son wrote that, after less than a three-day acquaintance, he planned to marry an American girl named Jennie Jerome.

The Duke was keenly disappointed. A marriage at this time would interfere with young Lord Randolph's campaign for a seat in the House of Commons. Moreover, the Duke strongly disapproved of the speed with which the engagement had been made.

After investigating Miss Jerome's background, he was even more disturbed. Her father was a newspaper publisher and gambler who had made a fortune on Wall Street and squandered lavish sums on entertainment, horses and the opera. The Duke disapproved whole-heartedly of such a way of life.

Eventually the unhappy situation was resolved to everyone's satisfaction. Lord Randolph complied with his father's wishes and delayed his wedding until after the election. And when the Duke met Miss Jerome he was most impressed by her dark beauty and good manners, and gave his consent to the marriage.

The year 1874 was an eventful one for Lord Randolph—he had been elected to Parliament, and he had married the girl he loved. Then, on November 30th, his first son, Winston Leonard Spencer Churchill, was born at Blenheim, the ancestral estate of the dukes of Marlborough.

Two years later the Duke of Marlborough was appointed Lord-Lieutenant of Ireland by Prime Minister Benjamin Disraeli. The Churchills consequently moved to Dublin, where Lord Randolph acted as the Duke's secretary. It was in this role that he first showed signs of his brilliant talent for politics.

Winston's earliest memories are of these Dublin years. While his father was busily involved in advancing his political career, Lady Churchill was equally busy giving large dinner parties and fancy-dress balls. They were a very attractive and much-sought-after young couple, who preferred the pleasures of a gay social life to a quiet domestic one. As a result, Winston was really brought up by his nurse, Mrs. Everest, whom the boy grew to love dearly.

Lady Randolph Churchill.

It was Mrs. Everest who put the little red-headed boy to bed every night and listened to him say his prayers. It was also Mrs. Everest who tried to teach him his ABC's and simple arithmetic. One of the first books Winston ever owned was a present from Mrs. Everest, called *Reading Without Tears*. But the pug-nosed, freckle-faced little boy hated to study. It seemed such a waste of time when he could be riding his donkey or playing war games with the red-coated toy soldiers which were a gift from his father.

The Churchill family returned to London early in 1879. The following year the Liberal party came into power, led by the new Prime Minister, William Ewart Gladstone. Winston's father, Lord Randolph, who was a member of the Conservative opposition, decided to plunge into politics, and in a few short years he became a leading figure in British political life.

Winston was now seven, and it was time for him to be sent to school. His father selected St. James's, one of the most fashionable and expensive preparatory schools in England.

Winston hated St. James's. He bitterly resented being forced to study Latin, and he did not much care for group games. He also stubbornly refused to learn subjects that did not interest him. As a result, the rebellious boy was frequently punished with severe beatings. His only entertainment was to read books of his own choosing rather than those forced upon him by teachers. When he was nine and a half his father gave him a copy of *Treasure Island*, which he read and reread with the greatest pleasure.

Strangely enough, Winston, who would grow up

Winston Churchill as a boy.

to become a remarkably powerful man, was a sickly child during his early school days. After two unhappy years at St. James's, the Churchill family doctor suggested to Lady Churchill that the boy be taken out of the school. The doctor recommended a small school at Brighton, the British seaside resort, where Winston could continue his studies and regain his health at the same time. The school was run by two ladies who treated their young charges with kindness and understanding. Winston was permitted to study his favorite subjects, history and French, and encouraged to develop his outstanding facility for memorizing poetry. Riding and swimming, which Winston loved, were also included in the curriculum. Soon he became a healthy young boy again.

During the three years Winston spent at Brighton, his father made spectacular advances in his political career. Lord Randolph had been appointed Secretary of State for India in 1885, and in 1886 he became Chancellor of the Exchequer—the second highest political position in England.

When Winston was twelve his father decided it was time for him to go to Harrow, one of the great historic public schools of England. In England the term "public school" has just the opposite meaning from ours. It is really a very expensive private school attended mainly by the children of wealthy or titled families.

Winston's entrance examinations were a dismal

failure. He was unable to answer a single question in the Latin test, so he simply turned in a blank sheet of paper smudged with ink stains. His name was written at the top of the sheet. Dr. Welldon, the headmaster, took a very dim view of this applicant's academic possibilities. Nevertheless he was well aware that Winston's father was one of the most brilliant and powerful men in England. So the headmaster decided to take a chance. Surely the son of such a distinguished father must have some of his father's qualities. Winston was admitted to Harrow, where he spent four and a half years, finishing each year at the bottom of his class.

Winston never did master Latin and Greek, but he developed a real passion for English grammar and literature. And when the boy was truly interested in a subject he absorbed it thoroughly. His phenomenal talent for committing to memory long passages of anything he enjoyed reading began to emerge soon after he entered Harrow. For example, Winston recited 1,200 lines of Macaulay's *Lays of Ancient Rome* without a single error. For this he was awarded a prize. The only other prize he ever won at Harrow was the public school championship in fencing.

Winston absolutely refused to conform to school rules and regulations and that, combined with his intense hostility to education, did not endear him to his teachers. Nevertheless, he became very popular with his schoolmates. His fluency in expressing his ideas and his familiarity with the facts in a debate or discussion won him many admirers. But his tendency to get into mischief remained uncontrollable. In fact, this irresistible need for adventure almost cost him his life at the age of fifteen.

A deserted old house in the town of Harrow was reputed to be haunted. In the large overgrown garden surrounding it there was a dry well choked to the top with trash, the accumulation of many years of neglect. According to rumors circulated in the town, a passage led from the bottom of the well to the house. Winston thought it would be fun to find out if the story were true.

The only way to get to the bottom of the clogged-up well was to blow it up, and this Winston proceeded to do. He assembled a simple but effective bomb, about the size of a pumpkin. Then, with a perfectly innocent expression on his face, he walked through the streets of Harrow with the bomb tucked under his arm. When he reached the haunted house, he lit the fuse and dropped it into the well. Nothing happened. He leaned over to see what was wrong, and at that precise moment the bomb exploded.

Miraculously, he was not blown to pieces, escaping with only a blackened face and singed hair and eyebrows. A kindly woman who lived near by heard the roar of the exploding bomb and turned just in time to see a small boy ejected from the well. She

took him into her house and bathed his blackened
face. He thanked her and said ruefully that he expected to be expelled from school after this escapade.
However, dismayed and discouraged as Dr. Welldon
was by the unpredictable young Churchill, the headmaster permitted the boy to stay on and continue
his half-hearted studies.

A Cadet at Sandhurst

Winston's toy soldiers proved to be an influence that helped shape the course of his life. While the boy was still at home, Lord Randolph came to visit his son one day. Winston, eager to please his father, put his army of toy soldiers through a series of elaborate military maneuvers. Lord Randolph watched the performance thoughtfully. Finally he asked the little boy, "Would you like to go into the army?" Winston was thrilled by the idea.

At the end of his first year at Harrow, the boy's grades were still the lowest in his class. Reluctantly his father gave up any notion of Winston's following in his own footsteps. How could such a poor student ever pass the examinations for Oxford or Cambridge? Remembering his son's passion for playing at war, Lord Randolph asked him if he still was

Lord Randolph Churchill.

interested in the army. Winston, who was delighted to think that his father had discovered the seeds of military genius in him, said he was. The sad truth that his father considered him hopeless in any other field never occurred to the self-assured lad.

Thus, with his father's encouragement, Winston began to prepare for Sandhurst, the West Point of England. First he applied himself diligently to the required courses in army class at Harrow. The applicants for army class knew that one of the tests would be to draw from memory a detailed map of some country. The night before this test Winston put all the maps from his atlas into a hat, and then pulled one out. It was a map of New Zealand. Winston studied the map until he knew it thoroughly. The next day the head of army class announced that the first problem was to draw a map of New Zealand. Winston was in luck! And his superb memory did not fail him, down to the last obscure stream and railroad line in that little-known country. Winston passed the test successfully and was admitted to army class.

In order to qualify for Sandhurst, a candidate had to take mathematics, Latin and English. Winston chose, in addition, French and chemistry. He really tried hard but, although he was able to limp along in the other subjects, he never could master mathematics. He took the Sandhurst entrance examinations twice and failed both times.

In despair, Lord Randolph Churchill took his son out of Harrow and sent him to a tutor who specialized in preparing boys for Sandhurst. With his third try, Winston just barely made it. He was accepted at Sandhurst. The boys who came out on top were destined for famous infantry regiments; those with low grades would end up in the cavalry. Naturally Winston found himself assigned to the cavalry, but he didn't mind a bit. He had always loved horses and riding.

Winston was just eighteen then. One of his aunts, Lady Wimborne, had invited the Churchill family to stay at her home in Bournemouth for the winter. While Winston was enjoying a brief holiday there before entering Sandhurst, a terrible accident almost killed him.

One day his younger brother Jack and a cousin suggested that they play a game somewhat similar to an American favorite, cops-and-robbers. Winston was to be the robber, and the other two were to pursue and capture him. The chase was an exciting one across rather wild terrain. Suddenly Winston found himself trapped on a narrow bridge which crossed a deep ravine deceptively thick with fir trees. At either end of the bridge were his pursuers. Winston decided he could avoid capture by leaping off the bridge onto the top of the closest tree. His plan was to break his fall by jumping from branch to branch in his descent. Unfortunately he went straight on down, twenty-nine feet to the ground.

The terrified boys ran back to tell Lady Churchill. Winston lay unconscious for three days while some of the best doctors summoned from London hovered over him. Among his numerous injuries was a ruptured kidney. For a long time Winston wavered between life and death, but gradually he began to improve. He remained bedridden, however, for nearly the entire year of 1893.

Winston was brought back to London for the

long period of recuperation. During this year he met some of the most famous members of Parliament. They came to luncheon or dinner at the Churchill home, and the boy would listen avidly as these brilliant political leaders discussed the news of the day. Not all of the guests were colleagues of Lord Randolph, but even those who were bitter political antagonists showed a mutual respect and courtesy that impressed the young invalid for the rest of his life.

As soon as he was able to get about, Winston was taken to the House of Commons to listen to some of the great debates. What fascinated the boy most about the procedure of the House was that a member might make a fierce speech attacking an opponent and then, when the session was over, engage him in the most friendly conversation.

It had been a disappointment to Lord Randolph when his son failed to qualify for one of the country's famous infantry regiments. And, it was going to be costlier than he had expected to maintain Winston in the officers' school. When sons of aristocrats were sent to the Royal Military College at Sandhurst, the family usually provided a "batman"—a sort of soldier-servant—to attend the young officer. Because Winston was to be in the cavalry, his father would have to provide not only a batman but a horse as well!

Despite his father's gloomy view of the future of a cavalry officer, Winston could not conceal his de-

Churchill (left) and two companions at Sandhurst.

light at the prospect. And because he cared deeply
about proving himself at Sandhurst, he applied his
keen intelligence to the subjects he now had to study.
These included tactics, fortifications, map making,
military law and military administration. In addition he learned to shoot, to blow up bridges and to
dig trenches. He learned to ride in a disciplined manner. For a while he did not care much for drill and
was put in the awkward squad to sharpen up. Eventually he became an excellent rider and wrote in his
recollections of his early life: "Horses were the greatest of my pleasures at Sandhurst."

Winston's profound interest in all things military
was shown in the collection of books he began to
acquire. He bought books on all aspects of warfare
and military history and read them over and over
again. So eager a student had he become that he
managed to get himself invited to dinners at the
Staff College, where senior army officers were being
trained for the high command. He would sit entranced
listening to the officers discuss supplies, communi-
cations and strategy. Winston's interest and per-
severance paid off. At the end of two years, he was
graduated with honors from Sandhurst, eighth in a
class of one hundred and fifty.

In 1895 Winston suffered two severe tragedies.
His father died in January and, toward the end of
that same year, his beloved old nurse, Mrs. Everest,
passed away. He was by her bedside when she died.

After Lord Randolph's death, Winston's mother became active in promoting her son's career. She was still a great beauty, and her influence reached to the highest court circles. She and her son drew extremely close and established a deep bond of affection, which lasted until her death in 1921.

In March, 1895, Churchill received his commission in the 4th Hussars, a crack cavalry regiment composed of gentlemen-soldiers who played at war in the barracks and played equally hard at enjoying themselves in the rich, gay social world to which they belonged.

In those days newly commissioned officers were given a recruit's training for six months. Churchill, even though an officer, drilled with the regular troops and received the same rugged instruction and training that they did. Very soon he developed into a hard-muscled, confident cavalry officer.

Winter leave was approaching, and Churchill began to look around for a war—any war, any place, in which he could practice soldiering for a short time. As it happened, there was a revolt in Cuba against Spain. Using all his family connections, he obtained permission for himself and another subaltern, Reginald Barnes, to depart for Cuba. Other old friends high in the British diplomatic service wrote to the authorities in Spain, who replied that the son of Lord Randolph Churchill, as well as his friend Reginald Barnes, would be made welcome when they arrived in Cuba.

Next Churchill went to see the editor of the London *Daily Graphic* and offered his services as a foreign correspondent—for a fee. The editor signed up the brash young man and agreed to pay him twenty-five dollars for each article he sent in.

Early in November, 1895, the two eager young officers sailed to New York, and there boarded a boat that took them to Havana. The letters of introduction carried by Churchill and Barnes produced a cordial welcome from Spanish authorities in Havana. Arrangements were made for the two British officers to travel out to Santa Clara, where they were greeted by Marshal Martínez Campos, head of the Spanish army. Marshal Campos turned them over to a young lieutenant, Juan O'Donnell, who spoke perfect English. They told O'Donnell that they were anxious to see some action. The Lieutenant warned them that the enemy was all around, invisible but dangerous. The Cubans were fighting a guerrilla war, hiding in the steaming jungles, sniping and swooping down in surprise attacks.

O'Donnell accompanied Churchill and his friend Barnes to the town of Sancti Spíritus. It took them three days to make the 150-mile trip to the headquarters of General Suarez Valdez. Arriving in Sancti Spíritus at the height of a raging epidemic of yellow fever and smallpox, they were glad when the army moved out two days later to attack the Cuban rebels. (The Spaniards called them rebels, but the Cubans called themselves patriots who were fighting to liberate Cuba from the domination of Spain.)

"Officially you are merely observers from a friendly nation," Churchill and Barnes were told. "According to the rules of warfare, you cannot take part in the actual fighting, except in self-defense." Each of them was issued a revolver and a horse and outfitted with uniforms which bore no insignia.

The long Spanish column of 3,000 infantry, two squadrons of cavalry and a mule battery left the disease-ridden city at four o'clock in the morning and traveled for five days through lush, tropical country without a sign or sound or sight of war. On November 30th, the men were straggling slowly through an early-morning, low-lying fog when they were ordered to halt for breakfast. Everything was perfectly still, yet the air seemed to vibrate with danger. Suddenly a volley of shots shattered the stillness. A horse tethered to the tree against which Churchill was resting whinnied and fell dead. The bullet that killed it had passed only a foot above Churchill's head.

The day was November 30, 1895. Churchill had received his baptism of fire on his twenty-first birthday.

Recovering from the surprise rebel raid, the advancing Spanish army continued to follow an uncertain trail through the forest and soon came upon a cold, fast-flowing river. Churchill and Barnes persuaded two Spanish officers to join them for a swim. After a pleasant dip, the four men were dressing on the bank when they heard a shot fired very close to them. Then more bullets went whizzing over their heads. The young men hurriedly completed their dressing and sped back to headquarters.

This kind of guerrilla attack kept up for the next five days. The Spanish general ordered a retreat when he realized that his forces had almost exhausted their ammunition and had only one day's food rations left. They withdrew to a town called La Jicotea until they could replenish their supplies. Soon after, Churchill and Barnes left Cuba and returned to England.

Churchill's dispatches to the *Daily Graphic* began to appear in London on December 6th. His articles were extremely well written, and aroused quite a bit of interest. So far as the London press was concerned, Winston Churchill was the only correspondent who had seen any action in this particular war. With an amazing foresight for such a young man, he prophesied that Spain would never win a quick victory over the Cuban patriots. His prophecy turned out to be correct.

Polo and India

Not long after young Churchill's return from Cuba, the 4th Hussars received orders to sail for India. The word came in the spring of 1896, and the officers of the regiment were given six months in which to arrange their affairs. Assignment to India meant a stay of at least twelve to fourteen years, so the young officers took fullest advantage of their six-month leave.

For Winston Churchill that half-year was one of the happiest times in his life. A modest income left to him by his father enabled him to buy five fine polo ponies. He lived at home with his mother and played polo two or three times a week. He had become a tall, slim, highly skilled athlete. The 4th Hussars' polo team seldom lost a match.

Churchill also devoted himself to the amusements

of the social world. As a descendant of the dukes of
Marlborough and as the son of the famous Lord
Randolph Churchill, young Winston was received
warmly in the most aristocratic society. He was a
frequent guest in magnificent palaces and historic
old town houses. If the Duchess of Devonshire needed an extra man at her dinner table, she would in-
vite the handsome young officer.

Through his Aunt Lilian, widow of his uncle, the
eighth Duke of Marlborough, Churchill met a man
whom he came to admire enormously. Lilian had re-
married, and her new husband, Lord William Beresford, seemed to embody all the qualities that young
Churchill held most desirable. An immediate and
lasting affection developed between the two men,
despite the difference in ages. On one occasion at
the Beresfords' country house Churchill made the
acquaintance of Sir Bindon Blood, an almost legendary fighter in the Indian campaigns. The stories of
Sir Bindon's adventures in India impressed the eager
young warrior so much that he asked General Blood
if he could serve under him in any future Indian
uprising. General Blood promised he could.

In September the 4th Hussars set off from Southampton for India in a troop ship carrying about
1,200 men. The journey from England to India took
twenty-three days. Finally the ship dropped anchor
in Bombay Harbor, where small boats were available

to take some of the officers ashore. The boat in which
Churchill rode came alongside a big stone pier. Shal-
low steps were carved into the stone, and iron rings
for hand holds helped the arrivals get a footing on
the steps. As Churchill reached up for one of the
iron rings, a heavy swell pulled his small boat away
from the pier and he was left dangling from one iron
ring. He felt a sharp pain in his right shoulder but
managed to grasp another ring with his left hand.
Finally his feet found the steps. When Churchill
reached the top of the pier, his right arm hung in a
strangely twisted position. He had dislocated his
shoulder.

The results of this injury stayed with him for the
rest of his life. The shoulder had a curious way of
popping out of joint at the most unexpected times.
He could never play tennis again, and for years he
had to give up swimming, a sport he really loved.
His polo playing was also affected, and even such a
small gesture as raising a glass to his lips, or stabbing
the air to emphasize a point while talking, could
wrench the shoulder out of place again.

Two days after their arrival in India the 4th Hussars were sent to a rest camp at Poona and then on
to Bangalore, where the regiment was to make its
headquarters. The army made no provision for the
officers' living quarters. The custom was to grant
a rent allowance to each officer. This allowance, together with his regular pay, enabled him to share

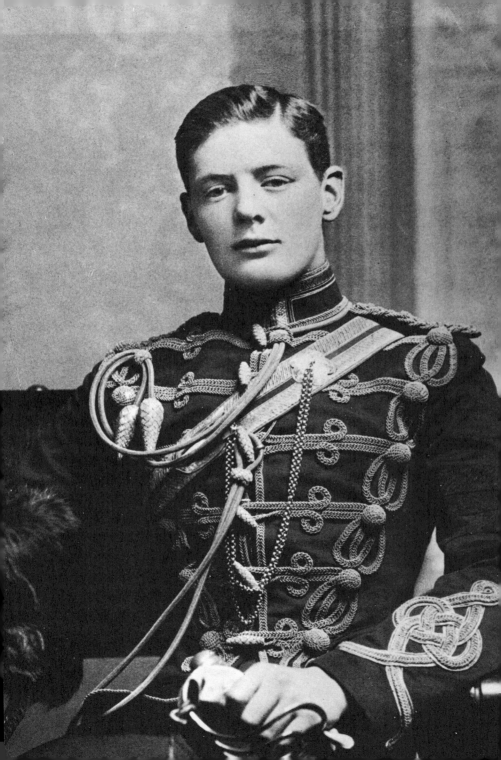

the expenses of a bungalow with two or three other
officers. The bungalows were not far from the cavalry headquarters. They were cool, one-story high,
and stood in their own gardens surrounded by a
high wall. Churchill, his old friend Reggie Barnes
of the Cuban adventure, and another officer took a
spacious four-room bungalow.

It was a wonderful time and place for an ambitious and daring young officer. At the moment, however, there were no rebellions to be crushed, so the
4th Hussars settled down to the second most important thing in the world for them—polo. All the
officers, whether they played or not, contributed to
a fund which enabled the regimental polo club to
buy a stable of twenty-five ponies for their four-
man team. Even with his permanently injured shoulder, Churchill was a superb polo player. With the
same skill and fierce determination he applied to
everything that interested him, he helped lead his
team to the championship by defeating the former
champions, the 19th Hussars. The 4th Hussars' polo
team became the champions of India.

Of course there were daily military duties of a
minor kind, such as early-morning parade, drill and
maneuvers for about two hours. By noon the heat
was so intense that the men had to seek shelter in-
doors, out of the scorching sun. After lunch they
took a long siesta until five o'clock. That was the
hour for which the officers had been waiting all day

Winston Churchill in the uniform of the 4th Hussars.

—polo practice began with the shadows of late afternoon.

For a man of Churchill's great but as yet undeveloped intellectual capacities, this daily afternoon nap became a bore. Suddenly it occurred to him that he was sadly lacking in any knowledge in the subject areas of history, philosophy and economics. With typical Churchill enthusiasm he plunged into an intensive program of reading and study, and spent the long afternoon hours filling the gaps that Harrow and Sandhurst had never been able to penetrate. He devoured dozens of major and minor works, and his amazing memory retained all that was important and useful.

One of the first giants Churchill tackled was Gibbon's *The Decline and Fall of the Roman Empire.* "I rode triumphantly through it from end to end and enjoyed it all," he later wrote. After Gibbon he read numerous other English historians, essayists and poets. He discovered Darwin's *The Origin of the Species* and Plato's *The Republic.* Bartlett's *Familiar Quotations,* one of the books he memorized practically in its entirety, Churchill found very useful many years later in his verbal battles in the House of Commons. With one apt quotation from the famous classic he could demolish an adversary.

In the spring of 1897 Churchill was able to get a three-month leave to go home. While enjoying him-

self in London he read in the papers of the revolt
of the Pathans, a particularly savage tribe living on
the North-West Frontier of India. The newspapers
also mentioned that Sir Bindon Blood would command the forces sent to put down the rebellion.

Here, at last, was a chance for action!

The first thing he did was to telegraph General
Blood reminding him of the promise he had made
to Churchill at the Beresford home. Then he caught
the first available boat for India to report to his regiment. When the ship docked at Bombay, Churchill found a message from the General: "Very difficult; no vacancies; come up as a correspondent; will
try to fit you in. B.B."

Churchill lost no time in calling on the editor of
a local paper, the Allahabad *Pioneer*, and easily
talked the newspaperman into putting him on the
staff. Churchill's mother, who was being kept informed by wire, used her influence in London to get
him an appointment as war correspondent for the
Daily Telegraph. Thus armed with assignments from
two newspapers, Churchill approached his command-
ing officer and wheedled an extended leave to cover
the fighting.

That same night Churchill went to the Bangalore
railway station and bought tickets for Nowshera—
the railhead of the Malakand Field Force. Soon he
was on his way.

Sir Bindon Blood was away in a neighboring val-

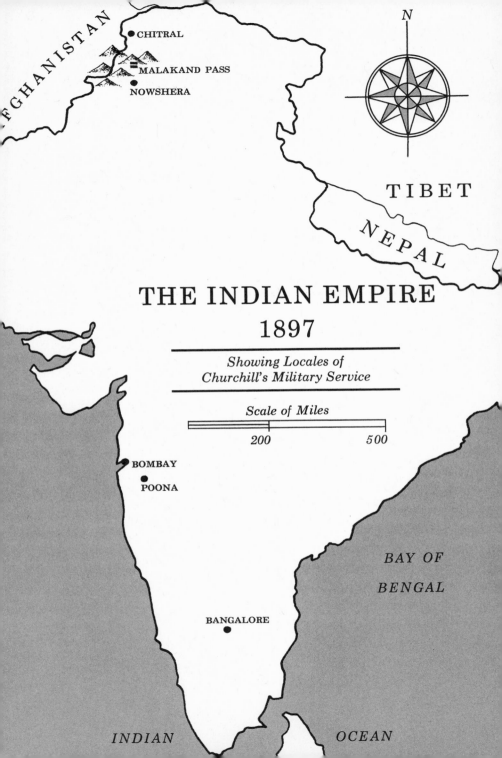

ley subduing another rebellious tribe when Churchill
arrived at his destination. While he waited for the
General's return, the officers of the Malakand Field
Force told him what the fighting was about.

Three years earlier, British troops had seized and
held the summit of the Malakand Pass. This was
considered a point of great strategic importance,
overlooking as it did the roads leading to the Swat
Valley and the great road leading to Chitral. The
Indian tribesmen naturally resented the British in-
trusion, since they had lived in the area for centuries
and considered it their private domain. They looked
upon the British as aggressors and proceeded to
snipe away at them with a vengeance.

At headquarters Churchill was told officially that
he was not a soldier in this campaign; he was only
a war correspondent. This meant that he had to
pay his own expenses. He was able to acquire some
military equipment formerly owned by soldiers who
had been killed in battle. He also bought two horses
and hired an Indian batman to serve as a combina-
tion valet, groom and cook. By the time the troops
who were fighting in the valley returned to headquarters, Churchill was ready to join them.

Under Fire in India

Warfare in the high mountain valleys of India was quite different from maneuvers and drill at Bangalore, as Churchill was soon to find out. His very first night in the field was disturbed by gunfire from Pathans hidden on the outskirts of camp. As soon as it was dark, the tribesmen crept close to the British forces and began firing at them. Campfires which had been lit to prepare the evening meal for the troops gave the Pathans a perfect view of their target. The British had no such advantage, for the tribesmen were hidden not only by the darkness but also by trees and heavy shrubbery. A few men were wounded but no serious damage was done.

The following day the British troops, divided into three brigades, continued their advance. When one of the brigades pitched camp toward nightfall, it was attacked by frenzied natives, who seemed to spill out of the craggy slopes surrounding the encampment. At the end of three hours of continuous firing, forty British soldiers had been killed. The Pathans slaughtered numerous horses and pack animals as well.

General Bindon Blood was so angered by this action that he decided upon immediate reprisal. He ordered the commander of the second brigade, General Jeffreys, to advance into the valley and destroy all the crops, blow up water reservoirs and any castles in sight.

"If you want to see a fight," Sir Bindon told Churchill, "you may join Jeffreys."

Churchill was delighted. The next day he rode in with an escort of Bengal Lancers who happened to be joining the second brigade. When they arrived at General Jeffreys' camp, Churchill saw that adequate preparations had been made for the protection of the men and the animals.

At dawn the next day the entire second brigade, preceded by a squadron of Bengal Lancers, marched into the Mamund Valley. General Jeffreys ordered his men to separate into three detachments. Each detachment, in turn, was divided into groups of approximately twenty men. In this way the whole second brigade, comprising 1,200 men, was spread out across the wide valley.

Churchill attached himself to one of the forward

cavalry groups. As they galloped toward the head
of the valley, the entire area seemed deserted. Not
a shot was heard. Through their field glasses, however, the men could see a village perched crookedly
on a distant hill. Tiny figures were scurrying about
holding aloft swords that gleamed in the sunlight.

The officer in charge of Churchill's group ordered
the men to dismount and tether their horses. An
infantry detachment was supposed to be following
on their heels to give support.

The men took cover in a little grove and opened
fire. Suddenly the whole mountain seemed to come
alive. Tribesmen, hidden two thousand feet above
the British, answered the attack with volley after
volley of gunfire.

When the infantry finally appeared, Churchill decided to join a detachment of soldiers assigned to
climb the mountain and capture the village. By the
time they reached their objective, they found that
the village was deserted. Some of the men poked
around in the little mud houses; others just sat and
rested after the exhausting climb. Suddenly wild
cries and shrieks broke the stillness, and Pathans
began to drop from the crags above, shooting as
they descended on the British troops. Churchill,
who was supposed to be reporting the battle, not
fighting in it, borrowed a rifle and began to fire. Two
men in his group had been killed and three others
seriously wounded.

Wounded men were never left behind in Indian frontier fighting. Tribesmen invariably tortured and eventually killed any prisoners they captured— wounded or not. While the British were dragging their wounded to the rear, an incident occurred which enraged Churchill. He saw a savage tribesman rush up and slash at a helpless, wounded adjutant. Churchill whipped out his revolver and began to fire. He became so absorbed in the conflict that he did not realize the other British soldiers had retreated, leaving him alone with the enemy. Quickly he withdrew and, with well-aimed shots, helped hold off the screaming Pathans while the British retreated with their wounded.

The small bedraggled group reached the foot of the mountain, still carrying their wounded comrades. The colonel in command of the battalion ordered Churchill to summon another force of British soldiers located about a half a mile away. Churchill successfully fulfilled his assignment, and the company was saved.

For the next two months Churchill stayed with the army that was fighting what came to be known as the Frontier War. All during this time he was sending his reports on the fighting to the *Daily Telegraph* and the Allahabad *Pioneer*. Signed simply, "By a Young Officer," his articles became a sensation in the London newspaper world. Churchill had never thought of himself as a professional writer, but his ability and style had improved greatly since his reports on the Cuban war. He was beginning to show a real talent for writing.

Meanwhile, the commander of the 4th Hussars decided that the young officer had had enough leave of absence from his regiment and ordered his return to routine duty.

Back in Bangalore, Churchill found barracks life, with all its ease and comforts, quite dull after the Frontier War. To overcome the boredom he decided to write a book about his recent experiences. He collected all of his newspaper articles, added some new material and, in March, 1898, his *The Story of the Malakand Field Force* was published. When his publisher sent him his share of the profits, Churchill was amazed to learn that it was equal to two years of his pay as an officer. It was then that he began to think seriously of a career as a military writer covering wars wherever they broke out in the world. He made up his mind to resign from the army as soon as the trouble in India was over, and concentrate on writing.

But not all the reaction to *The Story of the Malakand Field Force* was favorable. High-ranking army officers in particular were infuriated by Churchill's audacity. With his incredible self-assurance, the young writer had described not only the battles he had witnessed but also those he had not. In addition, he had presumed to advise the British General

Staff on how to reorganize the army and how to conduct future wars.

Soon after the end of the Frontier War, word reached India that a British army under General Herbert Kitchener was gathering in Egypt for an attack on rebel forces in the Anglo-Egyptian Sudan. The Sudan, like Egypt, was part of England's vast African colonial empire. Some years earlier the British commander in the Sudan, General C. G. Gordon, had been murdered by religious fanatics called Dervishes. The Dervishes, who were perhaps the most savage and cruel fighters the British had ever encountered, had now worked themselves up into a full-scale war. And this time the British were ready to avenge the murder of General Gordon.

It was a popular cause, and every officer in India was eager for a chance to take part. Churchill promptly applied for a transfer to Africa and was just as promptly turned down. The man who stood in his way was General Sir Herbert Kitchener. Churchill's application to join the Anglo-Egyptian army had been approved by the War Office, but Kitchener wanted no part of him. He did not like young upstarts who wrote books that criticized and gave advice to the high command.

Churchill, however, was not going to accept defeat so easily. He obtained leave from his regiment and took the next boat to London. There he planned

Sir Herbert Kitchener, commander of British forces in the Sudan.

to use every possible influence—friends of his parents, relatives, anyone at all—in order to get to the scene of the fighting.

Lady Churchill tried every source and every connection to help her son. She even wrote to General Kitchener, whom she had known for many years, but his reply was a polite no.

Quite unexpectedly Churchill received a letter from the private secretary of Lord Salisbury, the Prime Minister. The Prime Minister had read his book on India and liked it. Would the author be good enough to come to 10 Downing Street to discuss Indian affairs at greater length with the Prime Minister? Would he! Churchill lost no time in acknowledging the invitation, and a few days later he was at 10 Downing Street, the residence of British Prime Ministers.

"I have been keenly interested in your book," Lord Salisbury told Churchill. "I have read it with the greatest pleasure and, if I may say so, with admiration not only for its matter but for its style. . . . I myself have been able to form a truer picture of the kind of fighting that has been going on in these frontier valleys from your writings than from any other documents which it has been my duty to read."

Churchill thanked him and politely rose to leave after about twenty minutes, but the Prime Minister kept him talking for more than half an hour. Lord Salisbury's parting words to him were, "If there is anything at any time that I can do which would be of assistance to you, pray do not fail to let me know."

The young author left 10 Downing Street with his head in the clouds. If anyone in England could break through Kitchener's obstinacy it was the Prime Minister. Several days later Churchill wrote to Lord Salisbury's secretary and asked him to put his case before the Prime Minister. His regiment had given him leave, the War Office had granted permission. Would the Prime Minister intervene in his behalf with Kitchener?

Lord Salisbury telegraphed the General. Couldn't Kitchener find a place for young Churchill? But Kitchener was a stubborn man. He still refused to accept Churchill as a regular army officer.

In the meantime an important piece of news reached Churchill. Sir Evelyn Wood, adjutant-general of the War Office, was also distressed by Kitchener's manner of selecting officers. The Adjutant-General's resentment offered Churchill an excellent opportunity. Through a friend he made certain that Sir Evelyn Wood was immediately informed of his problem.

Two days later Churchill received the following note from the War Department:

> You have been attached as a supernumerary Lieutenant to the 21st Lancers for the Soudan Campaign.

. . . It is understood that you will proceed at your own
expense and that in the event of your being killed or
wounded in the impending operations, or for any
other reason, no charge of any kind will fall on British
Army funds.

Churchill hurried down to the offices of the *Morning Post* and persuaded the editor to give him an
assignment as a war correspondent. This job would
at least pay his expenses.

Six days later he was in Cairo, headquarters of
the British Army.

The Defeat of the Dervishes

The 21st Lancers made the 1,400-mile trip from Cairo to the Sudan by boat and train. But the complicated journey was accomplished smoothly and on schedule. Exactly two weeks after they left Cairo the regiment arrived at headquarters, deep in the heart of Africa.

Churchill enjoyed the trip to the front although he was disturbed by a nagging worry. At any moment he expected a message to arrive from General Kitchener ordering him to leave Africa. But Churchill later learned that Kitchener had merely shrugged his shoulders upon hearing of the young officer's appointment. The General had far more serious matters on his mind. He was making preparations for what was to become one of the most spectacular battles in the history of British warfare—the Battle of Omdurman.

When General Kitchener's army moved slowly into the desert, Churchill was assigned to a squadron which rode not far behind an advance patrol. The mounted Lancers had an easier time of it than the infantry plodding along in the hot sands.

General Kitchener and his staff knew that the Dervishes, though not visible, were massed all around them. Occasionally they would spot an isolated rider tearing across the desert. On the morning of September 1, 1898, while Churchill's squadron rode slowly ahead searching the horizon, a young officer came riding up from the advance patrol and shouted, "Enemy in sight!"

The report was confirmed and immediately conveyed to General Kitchener. If the Dervishes continued advancing toward the British lines at their present rate of speed, battle was imminent.

Then, within a few hours, it was learned that for some unknown reason the Dervish army of 60,000 well-armed fanatics had stopped within three miles of the Lancers. Rumors that the Dervishes would attack that night began to fly up and down the British lines. As the troops settled down to an uneasy watch, orders went out that not a fire was to be lit or a shot fired.

The Dervishes made no move during the night, and a little before dawn the British troops began to stir from their fitful sleep. The silent encampment

came awake with the stir and excitement that pre-
cedes an impending battle. The River Nile, in the
background, was jammed with British gunboats.
The infantry and the mounted units were being de-
ployed into battle formation.

By 5:00 A.M. the 21st Lancers were mounted and
ready to move. Major Finn, Churchill's squadron
leader, had promised the young soldier-journalist
"a show" when the opportunity presented itself,
and he kept his word. Churchill was sent out in
charge of a patrol of six men and a corporal to find
out if the enemy was occupying a ridge about a mile
away. Quietly the horses picked their way up the
sandy slope. On Churchill's orders, one man rode a
hundred yards behind. This man could dash back
and report to Major Finn if the unseen enemy killed
or captured those who reached the crest first.

The patrol cautiously made its way up the slope.
Was the ridge held by the enemy? Were they riding
through the dawn straight into a trap set by an adversary wise in the ways of desert fighting?

As the patrol reached the crest of the ridge, the
early gray dawn gave a shimmering effect to everything—the sky, the sand and any possible life on the
desert stretching to the horizon. The men could see
a distance of three or four hundred yards across the
plain below them. There was not a sign of the enemy.

Suddenly the sun in all its glory skimmed above
the horizon. It was now possible to see a considerable

A group of British officers in South Africa, including General Kitchener (center of the first row) and Winston Churchill (second from left in the back row).

distance through field glasses. Churchill began to notice curious dark smudges scattered across the desert, mottling the gray sands. As bright sunlight hit them, the dark smudges came alive! Thousands of Dervish cavalrymen were riding swiftly forward, their swords, spears and rifles turned to mirrors by the reflecting sun.

Churchill dismounted and hurriedly tore a page from his notebook. "The Dervish army is still in position a mile and a half southwest of Jebel Surgham," he wrote, thus identifying his particular ridge to the commander in chief. Churchill handed the note to his corporal and instructed him to deliver it to General Kitchener.

Then he turned his attention back to the Dervish army. Swept away by the excitement of the scene, Churchill ordered his little patrol to ride down the slope to a point no more than 400 yards from the advancing enemy. There he gave the command to open fire. The enemy returned the fire, eventually getting too close for safety. The patrol was forced to beat a hasty retreat. As the men reached the top of the ridge, Churchill's corporal returned with an order from General Kitchener. "Remain as long as possible, and report how the masses of attack are moving."

Churchill's patrol remained on the ridge for nearly half an hour, exposed to the clash of arms from both sides. The British artillery opened with a barrage, and Churchill's men could hear the shells scream over their heads and burst among the Dervishes. At this point a message came up from Churchill's squadron leader ordering him to rejoin the 21st Lancers.

A cruel and vicious battle followed. The obsessed Dervishes fought with incredible bravery. Again and again they threw themselves fearlessly against the British infantry, as though human life did not matter at all in this conflict. By noon thousands of Dervishes had been killed. Then their surviving forces began to retreat, taking their wounded with them.

General Kitchener ordered a relentless pursuit of the fleeing Dervishes, and the British army began to move south toward the mud city of Omdurman. What the General did not know was that the left wing of the Dervish army had not yet been in the fight. Thus, just outside Omdurman, a force of some 15,000 men attacked the west wing of the British troops. A fearful clash took place as the opposing armies met. The 21st Lancers were ordered to charge.

Because of his weak shoulder Churchill slipped his sword into its sheath and decided to use his Mauser automatic pistol. He galloped into battle and was caught up in a nightmarish scene of wounded and dying men and animals. Bullets whistled all around him, and spears hurled by the enemy flashed past his head. A man riding behind Churchill was killed instantly. Within three minutes Churchill had killed two Dervishes and had perhaps wounded two others. Seventy Lancers had been either killed or wounded in the early minutes of the battle.

Shortly after the Lancers started their charge, the infantry arrived to complete the destruction of the Dervish army. The Battle of Omdurman was over.

Three days after the Battle of Omdurman the 21st Lancers were sent home to England. Churchill went with them. Back in London he lived at his mother's residence. He hated to depend on Lady

Churchill for financial support, but four years in the army had left him low in funds. Even when he could not afford it, Churchill had always been an extravagant young man. He never denied himself anything, whether it was a fine string of polo ponies or the best in food and travel.

The *Morning Post* paid Churchill more than £300 for his series of articles on the Battle of Omdurman. Obviously writing, which he enjoyed enormously anyhow, paid very well indeed. His news stories on the Sudan had attracted a great deal of attention, and his name was beginning to make an impression outside social and army circles.

Since Churchill planned to resign from the army before the year was up, he gave considerable thought to a writing career. As an author he would earn much more money than he ever could as a professional soldier. Besides, the opportunity for adventure and travel would be limitless.

Another possibility was a career in politics. During a visit to the Conservative party headquarters, Churchill was asked by a party worker if he would be available to speak at a few forthcoming political events. With a mixture of eagerness and apprehension, Churchill offered his services.

Winston Churchill made his maiden political speech in the city of Bath and, to his amazement, he was not a bit nervous. He was even more amazed when the audience cheered him wildly. The next day the

Morning Post printed his speech word for word and even published an editorial which proclaimed Churchill a new and exciting figure on the political scene.

Meanwhile the annual polo tournament to decide the championship of India was to be held soon. Putting aside all thoughts of a writing or political career, he set off for India and his old regiment, the 4th Hussars. Immediately after his arrival he joined his regimental team for two weeks of intensive training.

Unfortunately Churchill had a bit of bad luck the night before the team was to leave for the tournament. Walking down a stairway to the dining room, he slipped and dislocated his right shoulder again. He managed to put the shoulder back into place, but by the next morning he had practically lost the use of his arm. It was strapped tight to his side, and he knew from earlier experiences that he would not regain the use of it for at least three weeks. The young officer was bitterly disappointed. To cheer him up, his teammates urged him to try to play anyhow. He would not be able to hit the ball, but he could play a defensive game, "riding off" the opponent's offensive players.

Churchill played through the first two games of the tournament, both of which were won by the 4th Hussars. In the finals they had to meet the 4th Dragoon Guards. At the halfway mark the Guards were ahead two to one. Churchill was guarding their best player, Captain Hardress Lloyd. Lloyd roamed all

over the field with Churchill right beside him. Suddenly, in the middle of a confused scrimmage near the Dragoon goal, Churchill saw the ball rolling in his direction. He was barely able to lift his polo mallet to give the ball a feeble tap toward the goal. But by some miracle it went through the goal posts to tie the score. By the end of the match Churchill had made two more goals. Thus the 4th Hussars won the finals by a score of four to three.

Shortly after the polo tournament, Churchill resigned from the army. When he left India, his comrades in the 4th Hussars wished him well with a toast and a farewell dinner. He left behind many close friends whom he was never to see again.

Churchill engages in one of his favorite pastimes.

Capture and Escape

Churchill's farewell to the army and India gave his restless ambitions a chance to seek other outlets. During the voyage to London he spent most of his time in his cabin completing a book on the Nile campaign. Entitled *The River War*, it turned out to be a success with critics and public alike.

Back in London, Churchill decided to take a fling at politics. A special election, called a by-election, was being held in Oldham, Lancashire. The leaders of the Conservative party thought that this would be a good opportunity for Churchill to get some experience in politics by seeking a seat in the House of Commons. The young politician enjoyed the campaign but lost the election by 1,300 votes.

In the autumn of 1899 a war broke out in the South African Republic (Transvaal) and the Orange

Free State. Trouble had been brewing for some time in these South African republics between the Dutch settlers, who were called Boers, and the British. Suddenly the tense relations between the two groups of white settlers exploded into open warfare.

The British had come to South Africa later than the Dutch and were extremely dissatisfied with the way the Boers ran the government. The Boers, on the other hand, did not like British expansion and colonization in an area they considered Dutch. The hostility of the Dutch settlers was based on a simple economic fact: South Africa was fantastically rich in diamond and gold mines. Naturally the Boers did not care to let the British move in and take control of the territories.

The president of the South African Republic, Paul Kruger, did everything in his power to make things difficult for the British settlers. And the British, most reluctant to be forced out of a potentially rich area, began to send in more and more troops to protect their interests. President Kruger demanded that England withdraw her troops. Great Britain refused, and the war began.

Here was a wonderful opportunity for Churchill to exercise his talents as a war correspondent, and the *Morning Post* quickly took advantage of his availability. To his amazement he was offered a contract which guaranteed £250 a month, plus expenses, for covering the South African conflict. This

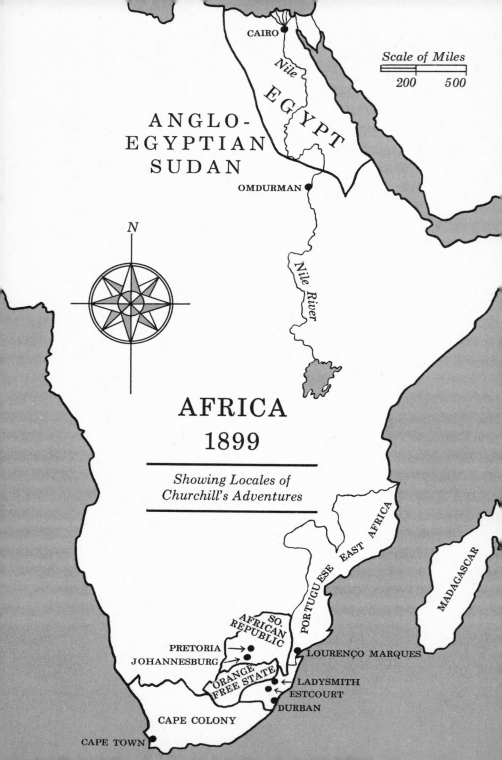

Scale of Miles
200   500

CAIRO

Nile

E G Y P T

ANGLO-
EGYPTIAN
SUDAN

OMDURMAN

N

Nile River

AFRICA
1899

Showing Locales of
Churchill's Adventures

PORTUGUESE EAST AFRICA

MADAGASCAR

SO.
AFRICAN
REPUBLIC

PRETORIA

JOHANNESBURG

LOURENÇO MARQUES

ORANGE
FREE STATE

LADYSMITH

ESTCOURT

DURBAN

CAPE COLONY

CAPE TOWN

was quite an extraordinary salary for a twenty-four-year-old reporter.

It was a long voyage from Southampton to South Africa, and Churchill's impatience for news about the war made the trip seem endless.

Immediately after landing at Cape Town he continued up to Estcourt, where the fighting was going on. There he learned that, far from being a short-lived colonial skirmish, this was going to be a full-fledged war. The Boers were more than holding their own; they were on the offensive on all fronts. These devoutly religious Dutch farmers were among the best mounted riflemen in the world, expert at guerrilla warfare. Moreover, they were completely at home in the South African plains.

An armored train carrying British troops was scheduled to leave for a mission near Ladysmith. At the invitation of Captain Aylmer Haldane, an old friend from India, Churchill climbed aboard the train just as it was leaving.

The train had traveled about fourteen miles when it was ambushed by the Boers. They had carried out a basic military maneuver by simply blowing up the tracks and derailing the train. Then, from hiding places behind boulders and trees, the Dutchmen poured murderous fire into the cars.

It was a short-lived battle. While Haldane and his men offered some covering fire, Churchill and a few volunteers labored to clear the tracks. Churchill hoped to put the locomotive and a few cars into working order. But to everyone's despair, only the locomotive with its tender succeeded in ramming free.

The Boers were now firing furiously, and it was apparent that an immediate retreat was imperative. The wounded were placed in the tender and cab of the locomotive. As the locomotive slowly steamed away, the other soldiers were ordered to follow alongside it for protection.

Although the wounded were successfully evacuated to Estcourt, the unfortunate soldiers who tried to make the retreat on foot fell behind as soon as the locomotive picked up additional speed. As a result, the Boers took more than seventy-five prisoners. One of them was Winston Churchill.

Churchill was herded off to an officers' prisoner-of-war camp at Pretoria. Even though he was well treated, he hated every minute of his confinement. He thought of nothing but escape from the moment he entered the prison. With Captain Haldane, who had also been captured, and another officer, Churchill considered possible plans for breaking out.

The odds were not good. Even if the men successfully climbed over the prison walls, they would still have to walk undetected through the city of Pretoria. Then they would have to travel approximately three hundred miles to reach Portuguese East Africa,

Winston Churchill (extreme right) and a group of British soldiers taken prisoner by the Boers.

the nearest neutral territory.

Finally the three prisoners agreed upon an escape plan. To put it into effect they waited for the first appropriate moonless night, which turned out to be the evening of December 12th.

Churchill was the first to flirt with danger. After clambering over the wall, he hid behind some shrubbery to wait for his companions.

An hour passed, and still there was no sign of

the two men. Since Haldane and the other officer had a compass and a map, Churchill desperately needed their assistance for a successful escape. As the minutes ticked away, he heard the voices of two British officers coming from behind the wall. He made his presence known, and was quietly informed that his two companions were under continuous surveillance by a suspicious sentry. Therefore Churchill was on his own.

He straightened his clothes and emerged from his hiding place. Tilting his stolen pastor's hat forward a bit, he walked calmly away from the prison grounds and into the city of Pretoria. Churchill knew not a word of the language and, without compass or map, he had to trust to luck for direction. Fortunately he located a railroad station on the edge of town. Concealing himself in a ditch, he waited until a freight train pulled into the station. He had no idea where the train was headed. He only knew that he must somehow reach Portuguese East Africa. As the train began to move out of the station into the darkness, Churchill hopped aboard and crawled into an open freight car piled high with empty coal sacks. Exhausted, he fell asleep immediately.

When he awoke at dawn the train was lumbering steadily through the wide-open countryside. Churchill was famished and began to nibble on one of the candy bars he had brought along. He decided that he had better jump off the train the moment it slowed down. It would never do to be found resting comfortably in a freight car. When the time came, he left the security of the freight car in one great leap and rolled into a ditch. Although covered with dirt he was all in one piece.

Hungry and thirsty, Churchill could see that he was near a native village. Since he had no way of knowing whether these natives would befriend an Englishman, he decided to hide out in a nearby woods until nightfall. As soon as it was dark he darted across the plain to a stream he had been eying longingly all day. He drank his fill, and then began to walk along the railroad line.

Churchill walked half the night, at times bogged down in waist-high swamps. Often he had to fight his way through tall sharp-edged grasses. Then suddenly he saw lights in the distance. Despite the risk involved, he decided to ask for help. He was simply too exhausted to continue.

As he approached the lights he could see a cluster of houses grouped around the opening of a coal mine. Churchill knew that many of the mines in South Africa were run by Englishmen, who had promised to continue mining operations during the war. For this service they were left unmolested by the Boers. Churchill's one hope as he staggered up to one of the darkened houses was that this was the home of such an Englishman. On the verge of collapse, he knocked on the door.

"Wer ist da?" a man's voice called.

Churchill shuddered with fear and disappointment. Had he stumbled right into the arms of the enemy?

As soon as the man opened the door, Churchill quickly explained that he was a Boer soldier who had fallen from a troop train.

The man studied Churchill for a few minutes, and then invited the bedraggled stranger into his home. In a small room the two men faced each other. After a long silence, the man requested more information about Churchill's accident. It was apparent to Churchill that his host was no fool. He decided to tell the truth.

After Churchill had finished talking, the man did not answer. His hesitation seemed endless. At last he walked slowly to the door and locked it. Then he turned and came toward Churchill, smiling and holding out his hand.

The man was an Englishman. Churchill had found the only house within twenty miles where he would not have been turned over to the Boers.

Journey to Freedom

The Englishman introduced himself as John Howard, manager of the coal mine. Many years earlier
he had become a naturalized Boer. Out of considera-
tion for his British birth he had not been called upon
to fight with the Boers.

Howard told Churchill that the entire country
was on the alert for him. The Boers were making a
house-to-house search up and down the railroad
line.

Churchill assured the mine manager that he did
not want to get him into any trouble. If Howard
would give him some supplies and perhaps a horse,
he would make his own way to a neutral territory.

Howard objected strenuously. He would enlist
the help of four other British subjects working at
the mine. With their assistance he would arrange

for Churchill's escape. After fetching some food for his guest, Howard went off to wake up his comrades.

John Howard returned to the house an hour later. "I have talked to the men," he said, "and they are all for you. We have decided that you had better sleep down in the mine, and tomorrow we will work out some plan to get you out of here."

Just before dawn Churchill and Howard walked to the entrance of the mine, where a big man named Charles Dewsnap was waiting for them. He turned out to be from Oldham, the town where Churchill had lost the election. "Don't worry," Dewsnap whispered, "they'll vote for you next time."

The three men entered the cage which took the miners down to their work. With breathtaking speed it shot to the bottom of the mine. Two more conspirators were waiting there with lanterns, a mattress and blankets. The little cluster of men began to weave their way through the narrow, twisting passages of the mine until they came to a wide, cool area. There the guides stopped and put down the mattress and blankets. After warning Churchill not to budge from his hiding place, the men departed with their lanterns. The accumulated fatigue and tension of the past few days caught up with Churchill, and he fell sound asleep almost at once.

Late the following afternoon John Howard brought the young fugitive a roast chicken and a few books. He told Churchill that the Pretoria government was in an uproar over his escape. As a result, Boer soldiers were combing the complete district to find the famous prisoner of war who had escaped so easily.

Considering the hue and cry raised over his escape, Howard thought it best for Churchill to remain in the mine for the next few days.

With only an occasional visit from one of the conspirators to break the monotony, Churchill spent the next two days alone in the mine. Then, on the evening of the 15th, Howard announced that he thought things were quieting down a little. To Churchill's delight he promised the young fugitive a walk on the plain later in the evening. That night Churchill also shifted his hiding place from the mine to the back of Howard's office, where he was concealed behind a stack of packing cases.

On the 16th, Howard explained the plan of escape. Not far from the mine there lived a Dutchman named Burgener, who was a secret British sympathizer. On the nineteenth of December Burgener was sending a shipment of wool to a seaport in Portuguese territory. Since the mine was connected by a branch line to the main railroad, the wool, packed in bales, would be loaded at the mine. This shipment offered Churchill a splendid opportunity to escape. The bales of wool would be arranged in one of the freight cars so that Churchill could conceal himself in a small opening in the center. Then a tarpaulin would be fastened over each one of the cars.

Howard thought it most unlikely that the bales of wool, protected by tarpaulins, would be examined very closely at the border.

On the afternoon of the 18th, Churchill heard the sound of gunfire and feared that the worst had happened. The firing continued off and on for about five minutes. Had Howard and his aides been shot for hiding him? He did not dare move from behind his barricade of packing cases, so he was in an agony of suspense until Howard walked into the room with a broad smile on his face.

"The Boer commander was here. No, he was not looking for you. As a matter of fact, he told me that they got you yesterday about a hundred miles from here. I didn't want him poking around in here, so I challenged him to a rifle match. We lined up some empty bottles and shot at them. He won two pounds from me and went away thoroughly pleased with himself. Incidentally, everything is fixed up for to-night."

Churchill was fully dressed and ready when Howard appeared at two o'clock in the morning for their rendezvous. Without a word he signaled to Churchill to follow him. They walked through the office to the siding, where the three freight cars were being loaded by natives. Howard sauntered over to the first car and pointed with his left hand. Churchill hopped onto the rear end of the car and saw that a space had been hollowed out for him between the bales of wool. It was just large enough for him to squeeze into. Then the tarpaulin was fastened over the bales, and the cars began to move.

A few hours later Churchill could see daylight between the floor boards of his car, and the loud banging and jerking indicated that the cars were being coupled to a train. They must now be on the main line. Gradually he began to relax.

As he groped around his tight headquarters, he discovered that he was not alone in his little nest. With him were two roast chickens, some slices of meat, a loaf of bread and three bottles of cold tea. It was more than enough to sustain him on his journey to the sea. There was also a loaded revolver, just in case.

The train rumbled eastward across the South African Republic until nightfall. Then it pulled into a station and was shunted off to a siding for the night. Despite his efforts to stay awake, Churchill fell into a deep sleep. The next morning he was awakened by the coupling noises of the cars being rejoined to the engine. Soon they were off again.

The train reached the border late that afternoon and slowed down to a stop. Churchill lay perfectly still, his heart beating wildly when he heard voices speaking in Dutch close by. Customs inspection! Would he be discovered? The train remained at the border for several hours, but nobody touched the

tarpaulin. Finally, sometime before midnight, the locomotive started to move again. When the train
stopped at the next station, he peeked through a
crack in his car and saw the most welcome sight in
the world—uniformed Portuguese officials. He was
in Portuguese East Africa! Before long his ride would
be over.

At his destination, Lourenco Marques, Churchill
crawled out of his hiding place. Dirty and dishev-
eled, he left the busy station unmolested. Outside
the gates the Dutchman Burgener was waiting for
him. After the two had exchanged glances, Burgener turned and walked down the street. Churchill followed not far behind. A few minutes later Burgener stopped and raised his eyes to the roof of a
building across the street. Following his gaze, Churchill saw the Union Jack fluttering gaily above the
British consulate! The man who had helped him escape then vanished.

When the British consul learned the identity of
his visitor, he was delighted. "We thought you were
dead," he told Churchill. "First, you will want a
shave, a hot bath, clean clothing and a good dinner.
Then I am sure you will want to send a story to
your paper. Please consider this your home."

After dinner Churchill went eagerly to work reading all the local newspapers. To his dismay he learned
that during his imprisonment the British had suffered a series of severe defeats at the hands of the

Winston Churchill after his escape from the Boer prison camp.

Boers. When he had finished with the newspapers, Churchill sat down to write a dispatch to his own paper.

The young man had no idea what a hero he had become at home. The English newspapers were filled with praise for his bravery in the armored-train incident. On top of this, the report of his escape, the long days of suspense and the conflicting stories of his death or recapture had made him a popular figure in England.

The British consul put him on a steamer to Durban, Natal, and there he received a tumultuous welcome. Bands were playing, and masses of cheering people awaited him as the boat docked. When he came down the gangplank, he was nearly torn to pieces by enthusiastic admirers. It was as though Churchill had won a major battle single-handed.

PART TWO

THE STORMY YEARS

*"I have a tendency against which
I should, perhaps, be
on my guard, to swim against
the stream. . . ."*

From War to Politics

Not all of England was overjoyed with the dazzling escapades of Winston Churchill.

His series of articles in the *Morning Post* criticizing England's poor military performance in the Boer War led to sharp attacks on the self-confident young correspondent. Among other things, he wrote in his articles: "We must face the facts. The individual Boer, mounted in suitable country, is worth from three to five regular soldiers. . . . The only way of treating the problem is either to get men equal in character and intelligence as riflemen, or, failing the individual, huge masses of troops. . . ."

Since Churchill was eager to return to action in the Boer War, he went off to see General Redvers Buller, whom he had known slightly during his four years in the army. Buller agreed to give him a

commission without pay as a lieutenant in a regiment known as the South African Light Horse.
Colonel Julian Byng, the commander of the regiment, made Churchill his assistant adjutant.

The war, which had been going so badly for the
British, gradually began to shift in their favor. In
February, 1900, the British Army finally lifted the
siege of Ladysmith, the city that had been encircled
by the Boers early in the war. The South African
Light Horse regiment took part in the relief of Ladysmith, and the squadron to which Churchill was
attached was one of the first to enter the city.

In June both Johannesburg and Pretoria were
captured by the British Army. Churchill partici-
pated in both engagements. And at Pretoria he had
the pleasure of witnessing the release of the men
he had known several months before as fellow prisoners of war.

Fortune had turned sharply against the Boers,
and the great battles were now over. The war was
no longer a news story for Churchill. He was permitted to resign his temporary assignment with the
South African Light Horse and return to England.

For the first time in his life Churchill was making
enough money to afford the luxurious life he loved.
High royalties derived from the rising sales of his
books and the ten months' accumulated salary from
the *Morning Post* left him extremely well off finan-
cially. Free of immediate money problems, Churchill

decided to return to Oldham, the scene of his first political defeat, and try once again for a seat in Parliament.

Oldham reacted quite differently this time to the ambitious young politician. During one speech to a packed and enthusiastic house, Churchill mentioned Mr. Dewsnap, the Oldham engineer who had befriended him during the Boer War. The audience cheered wildly. Although Churchill, a Conservative, was campaigning in a strongly Liberal district, he nevertheless won the election by a small majority.

Members of Parliament did not receive salaries in those days. Therefore Churchill decided that he had to accumulate as much money as possible before taking his seat. He made a successful lecture tour of England, which was later followed by a tour of the United States. His distinguished family background, combined with his reputation as a soldier and writer, attracted crowds wherever he appeared.

In February of 1901 Winston Churchill made his first appearance as a member of the House of Commons. The session opened with a debate on the Boer War. Churchill sat and listened to speaker after speaker. Disagreeing with many of the ideas expressed, he fervently wished that tradition would allow him to speak. (It is the practice in Parliament, as it is in the United States Senate, for a junior member to wait a few weeks or even months before making his first speech.) Churchill consulted several of the more experienced Conservatives. Considering his knowledge of the Boer War, would it be out of place for him to ask permission to speak? Some advisors suggested he follow tradition; others thought he should request such permission. Churchill, as usual, decided for himself.

Four days after he had taken his seat, he delivered his maiden speech in the House of Commons. Realizing that political careers can be made or broken by a first speech in the House, he had taken enormous pains to prepare his talk. He was to follow David Lloyd George, a Welshman and a Liberal who had risen from working-class beginnings to become one of the most brilliant and eloquent speakers in the House.

Churchill was extremely nervous as he stood up to speak. With the assistance of a Conservative ally, he had been able to revise his opening lines so that his speech followed smoothly after Lloyd George's. During his address, he defended the British position in the South African war, but at the same time paid tribute to the courage and fighting abilities of the Boers. Courageously he pleaded for a just and honorable peace for the Boers. At the close of his talk he paid a short tribute to his father.

The speech was such a success that many Liberals congratulated him. As a matter of fact, a lifetime friendship, frequently disrupted by sharp political differences, began between Churchill and Lloyd

Lloyd George and Winston Churchill.

George after this debate.

The former soldier and journalist approached his new career with a deep sense of responsibility toward his office. He had strong opinions, which he

expressed boldly. For example, he attacked the Conservative government on the questions of free trade,
the military budget and an honorable peace for the
Boers. By open support of Liberal policies throughout his first three years as a member of the House,
Churchill increasingly irritated and angered Conservative party leaders.

As the months of 1904 rolled by, the breach
widened between Winston Churchill and the Conservative party. Early in the year he lost the support of his own district. Although the Oldham party
leaders did not demand his resignation, Churchill
would certainly not have their support in the next
General Election.

Meanwhile, in the House of Commons, the majority of the Conservatives were united in their ·dis-
approval of the young dissenter. At times jeers and
catcalls drowned out his voice when he attempted
to speak. One day an incident occurred which has
never before or since been duplicated. Churchill
had begun a speech when Arthur Balfour, the Prime
Minister, rose from his seat and, followed by the
rest of the Conservatives, left the House. Shortly
after this incident, Churchill severed his connection
with the Conservative party and dramatically took
a seat next to Lloyd George on the Liberal side of
the House of Commons.

On December 5, 1905, the reins of government
passed into the hands of Henry Campbell-Banner-

man, leader of the Liberal party. His first act as
Prime Minister was to dissolve the Parliament and
schedule a General Election for the coming month.
In this election the Liberals won by a huge majority. Churchill retained his seat in the House by successfully running as the Liberal candidate in the
North-West Manchester district. (In England, a
member of the House of Commons does not have
to live in the constituency, or district, which he
represents.)

The new Prime Minister appointed the thirty-
one-year-old Churchill Under-Secretary for the
Colonies. Needless to say, some Conservatives were
furious. They felt, and a few of Churchill's friends
and family agreed, that he had betrayed his own
class for political ambition.

Despite his intense involvement in politics, Churchill found time during these early days of his political
career to write a two-volume biography of his father.
Some critics consider this biography, entitled *Lord
Randolph Churchill,* to be one of his finest works.

He also found time to meet, court and marry the
woman of his choice. At a house party in Scotland,
Churchill first met beautiful twenty-three-year-old
Clementine Hozier, the daughter of an old and
wealthy Scottish family. They fell in love and were
married on September 12, 1908. In the course of
time five children were born to the Churchills.

Meanwhile Churchill's political life was also un-

dergoing some drastic changes. From Under-Secretary for the Colonies he went to the post of President of the Board of Trade, a position similar to
the American Secretary of Commerce. In 1910 he
was moved to the Home Office, a branch of government which is responsible for such areas of public
welfare as immigration regulations, public works,
prisons and the London police and fire departments.

Churchill was a dynamic although controversial
Home Secretary. Under his leadership, a bill provid-
ing unemployment insurance was passed. He also
introduced legislation improving working conditions
for retail-store workers and coal miners. Remembering vividly his imprisonment during the Boer War,
he brought about needed prison reforms.

On the other hand, Churchill managed to arouse
the ire of labor. Toward the end of his term as Home
Secretary, he was required to put down a series of
violent dock and railway strikes that were sweeping
the country. To preserve order Churchill called out
the troops. As a result, demonstrations occurred
and a number of people were killed. For his part in
this bloodshed Churchill was bitterly denounced by
the unions.

At this time the friendship between Lloyd George
and Churchill flourished, and they competed regularly in delivering the most brilliant speeches to be
heard in the House. From the man in the street to
the top political leaders it was agreed that these

two remarkable young men had futures of luminous brightness ahead.

In 1911 Churchill became First Lord of the Admiralty, the British equivalent of the American Secretary of the Navy. Since the general European situation was becoming very tense, Churchill assumed his new post at an extremely critical time. There were widespread fears on the continent that Germany was preparing for aggressions beyond her borders. She had already had one skirmish with France over French rights in Morocco.

Winston Churchill was one of the first men in the British government to realize that war with Germany was not far off. He was convinced that Germany would attack France. With this in mind, he began to prepare for war shortly after he entered the Admiralty. He sent to the War Office a detailed report which amounted to a timetable of the future war and its duration. This historic document was prophetic in its accuracy. Unfortunately Churchill was looked upon with disfavor by several important military leaders, and the document was not utilized to its fullest.

A little later Churchill became interested in the development of some type of mobile, armor-plated and self-propelled vehicle to crush down obstacles and cross trenches; and eventually he had the satisfaction of seeing such a crude tank in action. He was also an enthusiastic advocate of the as yet prim-

First Lord of the Admiralty Winston Churchill with Viscount John Morley, a prominent figure in British politics.

itive airplane, envisioning a strong British air force.

But Churchill's duties at the Admiralty were not neglected while he was interfering so helpfully in what was strictly army business. In the few remaining years before World War I, he learned to the last detail every aspect of building and maintaining what was then the greatest fleet in the world. In the summer of 1914 the Royal Navy was going through an extensive test mobilization at Spithead. Churchill, with his uncanny sense of timing, ordered the navy to stay mobilized and be ready for action at a moment's notice.

World War I

Proof of Churchill's wisdom was not long in coming. When England entered the First World War on August 4, 1914, the superiority of the British Navy was undisputed. The Germans were not ready to participate in a full-fledged naval battle. Thus the Royal Navy was able to move the British Army to France without the loss of a single man.

As First Lord of the Admiralty, Winston Churchill surrounded himself with a group of excellent advisers, chief among whom was the retired Admiral John Fisher. This unusual man was over seventy years old when Churchill, against some opposition, called him back to the service. The two made a wonderful team despite the differences in their ages. Both men drove themselves mercilessly. Churchill ran his office on a twenty-four-hour-a-day schedule.

John Fisher (second from the left) and Winston Churchill, with two unidentified companions, on their way to an appointment.

Being a much younger man, he accommodated his hours to Admiral Fisher's, and between them they worked around the clock. They would leave each other dozens of messages—Fisher writing his in green ink and Churchill using red. More important, though, was the fact that they were both imaginative and bold at a time when many other men in the British high command were hampered by timidity and lack of foresight. Both Fisher and Churchill

knew that England could be vulnerable to air attack. Therefore one of the lasting results of this
unique collaboration was the development of the
Royal Naval Air Service, the forerunner of the present Royal Air Force.

During the first months of the war, the Allies—
including France, England and Russia—did not have
an easy time. The Russian armies suffered several
defeats on the eastern front, while the bulk of the
mighty German fighting forces pushed steadily toward Paris, forcing the British and French troops
to engage in a series of retreats. It was not until
September at the First Battle of the Marne that
the Allies scored their first decisive victory. This
victory destroyed any hopes the Germans harbored
for a quick, victorious end to the war.

After the First Battle of the Marne, Germany
turned her full attention on Belgium, which she
had invaded at the outset of the war. By October
the coastal city of Antwerp was severely threatened
by German forces. Here King Albert and the re-
mains of his Belgian army had retreated. With their
backs to the sea, they were on the verge of being
annihilated or captured by the Germans. Because
Antwerp was strategically located opposite the English coast, the Germans were determined to take it
at any cost.

On the evening of October 2nd, a meeting of the
British Cabinet was hastily called by Lord Kitchen-

er, head of the War Office. It was decided to do everything possible to relieve the beleaguered city. After the meeting Lord Kitchener took Churchill aside and asked if he would depart for Antwerp the following morning so he could personally evaluate the military situation. No urging was necessary. Churchill was delighted to accept the assignment.

Dressed in a naval fraternity uniform, he cut a weird figure as he met with King Albert and his Belgian general staff. Blissfully unaware of his amusing appearance, he soon became intensely involved in the military situation. In fact he even offered to resign his position as First Lord of the Admiralty and assume command of the Antwerp Allied forces. Prime Minister Herbert A. Asquith promptly refused Churchill's proposition.

On October 10th the Belgians finally surrendered. But their stiff resistance had proved invaluable to the overall war effort. By fighting a delaying action at Antwerp, they had tied down enemy forces and prevented German troops from forging an all-out offensive on other Channel ports. In the general confusion that followed, Churchill was held responsible for the defeat. The press and the public had to find a scapegoat, and they conveniently forgot that the decision to hold Antwerp had been made by the British Cabinet and not by Churchill alone. Churchill had also been sharply criticized for his extended stay in Antwerp. His critics felt his duties

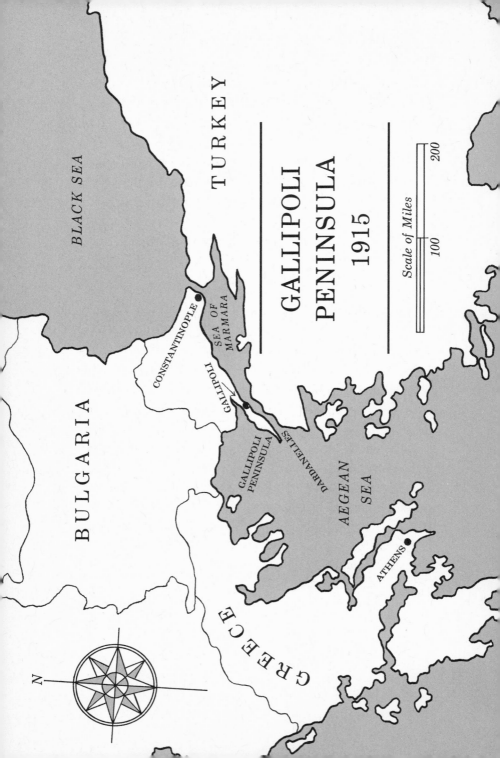

at the Admiralty had been slighted.

By the end of 1914 the war had reached somewhat of a stalemate. Although Paris had been saved
and Britain continued to dominate the seas, German forces were more than holding their own on
the continent. Churchill and other high-ranking
members of the British high command felt a new
offensive was needed, especially when Turkey entered the war on the side of Germany. The Turks
posed a definite threat to Russian forces in the region
of the Caucasus mountain range in southwestern
Russia.

Churchill and others began to develop a plan to
launch a massive naval attack on the Gallipoli Peninsula in eastern Turkey. Constantinople (Istanbul)
would be the principal objective. If the Allies were
victorious, they would be able to open up a supply
route to Russia, and Turkey would be cut off from
the central powers. Another major front would be
established. Success might also mean that uncommitted Balkan countries such as Greece, Albania
and Rumania—always bitter enemies of the Turks—
would enter the war on the side of the Allies. And
Italy, still wavering at that time, might be sufficiently impressed to join forces with the Allies, too.
The plan was unanimously approved by the War
Council on January 13, 1915.

Toward the end of that same month, Admiral
Fisher began to have grave reservations about the

British troops ready to disembark at Gallipoli.

Gallipoli campaign. Weren't they spreading themselves too thin? Wouldn't the welfare of the entire
British fleet be severely affected? Despite Fisher's
objections, plans for the campaign proceeded.

On February 19th the Gallipoli campaign got
under way when a fleet of British and French ships
opened a bombardment on the forts guarding the
Dardanelles, the strait leading to the Sea of Marmara
and Constantinople. The initial stages of the campaign were successful. In less than a month the outer
defenses of the Dardanelles were completely destroyed.

In the middle of March Churchill received a dis-
appointing telegram from Vice-Admiral Sackville
Carden, who was in command of the naval operations against the Turks. The Admiral informed
Churchill that he was ill, and that Vice-Admiral
John de Robeck, who was second in command, would
take charge of the operation.

A few days later Admiral de Robeck launched a
new offensive, which encountered trouble almost immediately—his fleet ran into a mine field and three
ships were severely damaged. De Robeck then called
a halt to the operation. On March 23rd Churchill
received a telegram from the Admiral stating he did
not think it advisable to continue with military
operations until the middle of April.

Churchill, greatly alarmed by de Robeck's decision, summoned his staff of admirals, including Ad-

miral Fisher. He showed them a telegram he wished to send to de Robeck. The telegram ordered him to resume action as soon as possible. The telegram was never sent by Churchill because Fisher and the other admirals refused to interfere with the admiral in charge of the operation. Instead, they insisted that the army take over and continue the campaign in Gallipoli.

Relations between Churchill and Fisher had been deteriorating for some time. Fisher, who had consistently supported Churchill's most unconventional views on warfare, began to feel that the First Lord of the Admiralty was really running the show by himself. As one of England's oldest and most experienced sailors, Fisher resented the supreme self-confidence and high-handed manner with which his younger colleague ran the Admiralty.

While the British high command wasted precious time debating the strategy for the Gallipoli campaign, the Turks strengthened and increased their defenses. It took Great Britain more than a month to gather enough troops for a large-scale invasion and transport them to the Dardanelles. The British attack, when it finally came, turned into a disaster. Thousands of troops were killed and wounded, and thousands more were taken prisoner. The Gallipoli campaign dragged on to become one of the worst defeats in the history of warfare.

During the crucial stages of the fighting, Churchill received a tremendous blow in the form of a letter of resignation from Admiral Fisher. It read:

First Lord.

May 15, 1915.

After further anxious reflection I have come to the regretted conclusion I am unable to remain any longer as your colleague. It is undesirable in the public interests to go into details—Jowett said, "never explain"— but I find it increasingly difficult to adjust myself to the increasing daily requirements of the Dardanelles to meet your views—as you truly said yesterday I am in the position of continually veto-ing your proposals.

This is not fair to you besides being extremely distasteful to me.

I am off to Scotland at once so as to avoid all questionings.

Yours truly,
FISHER

Fisher's resignation was painful enough for Churchill to take, but that was not all he was to suffer. The whole country turned in a terrible rage against Winston Churchill. Many people held him responsible for the thousands of lives lost at Gallipoli and demanded his removal from office. His popularity with the public reached one of the lowest points of his career.

The failure of the Gallipoli campaign and the resignation of Admiral Fisher had also created a furor in Parliament. Prime Minister Asquith was forced to form a coalition government containing many elements hostile to Churchill. Thus in May of 1915 Winston Churchill was forced to resign as First Lord of the Admiralty.

After his resignation, Churchill was asked to remain in the Cabinet, which he did until the following November. During those six months Churchill also retained a position in the War Council. This enabled him to continue to have a say in the conduct of the war. Then, in November, the War Council was reorganized and, to his acute disappointment, Churchill was excluded from the committee. Shortly after, he resigned from Prime Minister Asquith's Cabinet.

Since he had been rejected as a war leader, Churchill decided to rejoin the army as a fighting soldier. His naturally buoyant spirits revived at the prospect.

Not quite satisfied with the somber uniform of a major, he proceeded to add a little touch of his own— a sky-blue French helmet. Thus attired, he took off for France, where he was greeted with mixed feelings by the generals in charge. Fully aware of Churchill's tendency to take over leadership, they feared that he would take command of the entire military operation in France before they knew what was happening. A strict order from London directed that Churchill was not to get command of anything larger than a battalion.

After a month in the trenches, learning the rudiments of trench warfare, he was promoted to colonel and given command of the 6th Royal Scots Fusiliers. The Royal Scots became rather proud of their unusual commander. Certainly he was the only junior officer on the Western Front who managed to wine and dine his company commanders as though they were in a fashionable London club. He sent out men to scour the countryside for the best available food and wines. Frequently Churchill paid for these delicacies out of his own pocket. From declaring war on lice to introducing group singing whenever the men were in motion, he gave the Royal Scots a hilarious and busy time of it for the next six months. Cold resentment and suspicion had turned to affection and loyalty by the time Churchill left the trenches.

Churchill was still a member of Parliament, although an inactive one, while serving with the army. In the spring of 1916 he obtained leave to return to London in order to take part in a debate on the Royal Navy. He was made to feel most unwelcome in the House. Parliament had no use for him, and he became the victim of a constant stream of abuse and hatred from his political foes. His hands were tied while the military situation grew steadily worse.

It was during these critical days that he discovered painting. One day, while walking through the countryside, he came upon a man drawing some sketches. Churchill watched him for a while and became interested enough to buy paints, brushes and canvases. He discovered that painting could be an absorbing recreation. With his usual enthusiasm, he bought himself elaborate equipment, including a special outfit to wear at his easel. He loved painting landscapes in bold, vivid colors. Over the years he not only developed a considerable talent but also found painting his greatest form of relaxation.

But painting could serve only as relaxation for Churchill. Politics, as ever, continued to be his first love.

The political situation had been steadily deteriorating along with the military situation. Prime Minister Asquith was forced to resign and was replaced by Lloyd George, Churchill's old friend. When Lloyd George announced that he intended to have Churchill back in the government, there was such a vicious outcry from the Conservatives that he had to give up the idea. But after a while the savage attacks died down as one catastrophe followed another in the war. Lloyd George remained loyal to his friend, and eventually in July of 1917 he quietly offered Winston Churchill the newly created position of Minister of Munitions. The task of this ministry was to mobilize the nation's industry.

Churchill would once again be actively engaged in determining the course of the war.

Victory and Defeat

Throughout the first few years of the war raging in Europe, the United States had tried to remain neutral. But relations between Germany and the United States were becoming more strained each day. Then, in January of 1917, Germany declared a policy of unrestricted submarine warfare. Her U-boats were instructed to attack any ship traveling on the high seas, for it might be carrying food or arms for Britain.

During the first three months of unrestricted submarine warfare, more than eight hundred ships were sunk by German U-boats. Since American losses ran extremely high, antagonism toward Germany rose to a high pitch in the United States. On April 2, 1917, President Woodrow Wilson asked Congress to declare war on Germany.

Before long American troops began to pour into Europe. Equipped in many cases with arms supplied by Churchill's Ministry of Munitions, they provided the exhausted French and British forces with fresh man power to throw against the mighty German army. On November 11, 1918, a little more than a year and a half after America's entry into the war, Germany signed an armistice. World War I was over.

With the end of the fighting there was no further use for a Ministry of Munitions, so Lloyd George appointed Churchill Minister of War. As Minister of War, his immediate task was to see that the weary, homesick troops were returned to civilian life just as quickly as possible. He prevented near mutiny by ordering that the men be discharged on the simple policy of first in, first out.

Several months before the German surrender, Russia had collapsed under the impact of a revolutionary uprising which swept the country. The Czar was overthrown by a moderate group of revolutionists, who wanted to set up some form of constitutional government. Eventually, however, a radical revolutionary group called the Bolsheviks gained control and took over the central government. This Bolshevik government signed a separate peace treaty with Germany before the close of the war, so it would be free to concentrate its attention on internal problems. A counter-revolutionary group, including White

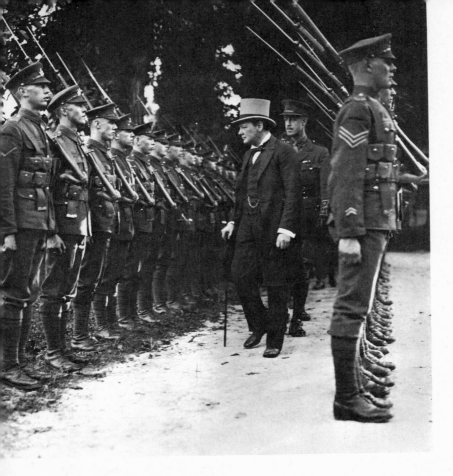

The Minister of War inspects British troops in Germany after the end of World War I.

Russians and others, were fighting the Bolsheviks. The Allies intervened half-heartedly with some support for the counter-revolutionaries. For a time they even maintained a limited number of troops in Russia. But their efforts were hindered by the disunity of the counter-revolutionary forces themselves.

When the victorious Allies finally met at Versailles to draw up a peace treaty, they were still united in their support of the anti-Bolsheviks but uncertain as to the exact amount of assistance they wished to offer. The world was weary of war, and after a time the Allied troops were withdrawn from Russian soil. Thus the counter-revolutionary movement failed, and the Bolsheviks remained in control of Russia.

Churchill, who abhorred the manner in which the Bolsheviks had assumed control of Russia, urged all-out military assistance for the White Russians and their allies. As Minister of War, he seized every opportunity to assist the struggling counter-revolutionary forces. Strong British public opinion against such intervention, however, eventually forced him to abandon the cause.

Meanwhile England was faced with a difficult situation in the Middle East. During the war large numbers of Arabs had fought against their rulers, the Turks, on the side of the Allies. For their co-operation the Arabs had received promises of independence and a nation of their own. But at the peace conference, after the war, their interests were for the most part disregarded. As a result, the Arabs were openly rebelling throughout the Middle East.

To cope with this problem Lloyd George appointed Churchill Secretary for the Colonies, relieving him of his duties as Minister of War. In turn, Churchill enlisted the assistance of the legendary Lawrence of Arabia and other expert advisers. After more than a year of negotiations, a satisfactory solution was reached—the Arabs would have the thrones of Iraq and Trans-Jordan (now Jordan). This masterly handling of a potentially dangerous problem pacified the Arab world for many years afterward.

While England was settling her affairs in all corners of the world, the people at home began to grumble about their government. As often happens after a major war, they were ready for a change. In 1922 a general election was held, and Lloyd George's Liberal government went down with a crash. The Labor party, a comparatively new political force, scored a tremendous victory.

During the general election of 1922, Churchill lost his seat in the House of Commons. The voters in the Dundee constituency, whom he had represented for quite a few years, felt Churchill had paid too much attention to international affairs and too little to the concerns of the district. Dundee was a working-class town and had become more and more radical since it first sent Churchill to Parliament.

At the very outset of the campaign, Churchill had a piece of bad luck which greatly hindered his

chances for reelection. The night before he was to
leave for Dundee to begin his series of rallies and
speaking engagements, he had to undergo an emergency appendectomy. No sooner was he off the critical list than he began to browbeat the doctors to
let him proceed with his electioneering. There was
no holding him down. Several days before the election, Churchill, with his stitches still in place, was
carried by stretcher to Dundee for some last-minute
campaigning. There he was transported by chair
wherever he went, and he had to make his speeches
sitting down.

His gallant try did him no good. As Churchill
himself said after the defeat at the Dundee polls,
"I am without an office, without a seat [in Parlia-
ment] . . . and without an appendix."

Thus Churchill, at the age of forty-seven, was
temporarily retired from the political arena. But as
usual his supreme self-confidence and naturally cheer-
ful spirits helped tide him through the empty days
that followed.

Immediately after his defeat at the Dundee polls,
he took his family on a holiday in the south of
France. It was here that he began writing *The World
Crisis*, a six-volume history of World War I. The
first two volumes of the history appeared in 1923,
and as volume followed volume during the next
seven years, Churchill received high critical praise
for his work.

Fortunately Churchill had inherited enough money to make it possible for the Churchill family to maintain their usual high standard of living. There was even enough money to buy Chartwell, a beautiful country home in Kent.

To amuse himself at Chartwell Churchill learned bricklaying and eventually applied for and received a bricklayer's union card. And, of course, he always found time for painting. Obviously Churchill was keeping busy, but he yearned to be back in the political limelight.

The political scene was changing constantly, and Churchill was disturbed to see the Liberal party aligning itself more and more with the Labor party. Nevertheless he ran and lost as a Liberal candidate in the general election of 1923.

Churchill's growing concern with the changing policies of the Liberal party and his two election defeats as a Liberal candidate forced him to make a drastic decision. After many years in the Liberal fold, he ran as an Independent in the 1924 general election. Again he lost, but the election results were encouragingly close.

Later that year Winston Churchill was finally reelected to the House of Commons. This time he ran as a Constitutionist candidate, but his backing came from Conservative quarters. Churchill was gradually returning to the ranks of the Conservative party.

In 1924 Stanley Baldwin of the Conservative

Chartwell, the country estate of the Churchill family.

party succeeded Laborite Ramsay MacDonald as Prime Minister. Once again, the Conservatives were in power. In this election the once-powerful Liberals disappeared as a major political party.

As a result of the change in government, Churchill achieved one of the greatest personal triumphs in his life. Stanley Baldwin appointed him Chancellor of the Exchequer, a post second only to that of Prime Minister. When Baldwin was asked why he had given this important office to the unpredictable rebel, Churchill, he replied: "Winston is the ablest mind in politics."

Churchill was very surprised by Baldwin's show of confidence in him. Moreover, the appointment had special significance. For it was a post that his father, Lord Randolph, had held, and it was in his father's robes that Churchill made his first speech as Chancellor of the Exchequer.

Churchill's problems in his new job were enormous. The man who had never been able to pass an ordinary arithmetic test at Harrow was now in charge of the economy of a whole country. It was his job to decide how much money was to be spent by the government and how that money was to be raised without hurting the country's prosperity. With enthusiasm Churchill plunged into straightening out matters about which his knowledge was sketchy indeed.

Upon the advice of his experts, Churchill restored

the gold standard and returned the value of the
pound to its prewar value. These measures had a
drastic effect upon the already shaky economy of
the country.

The coal mining industry was hit especially hard,
and the mine owners announced that, without a
wage cut or an increase in working hours, they would
have to cease operations. In rebellion the coal miners
threatened to go on strike. The government intervened in an attempt to resolve the conflict, but in
early May of 1926 the coal miners, along with Britain's whole unionized labor force, walked out in a
general strike. The entire economy of Great Britain
was paralyzed.

Churchill simply could not see the situation from
the workers' point of view, and everything he did
only increased their bitterness toward the Chancellor.

When the newspapers ceased publishing, Churchill was appointed by Prime Minister Baldwin to edit
a government paper called the *British Gazette*. It
was published in the building which housed the
offices of the *Morning Post*, the paper for which
Churchill had formerly written dispatches. For type-
setters, the new editor called on the trade schools;
for distributors, he called on the Automobile Asso-
ciation.

In eight days the sales of the *British Gazette* zoomed
close to the two million mark. Churchill wrote prac-

tically the entire contents of the eight-page newspaper himself. All the articles were violently anti-
labor, for the paper was frankly out to break the
strike. Churchill's activities aroused heated criticism
from newspaper publishers, Laborites in Parliament
and even members of his own party. What was the
Chancellor of the Exchequer doing editing a newspaper during a national emergency? the outraged
Laborites asked.

The general strike lasted for just ten days, but
the miners held out for months until they were literally starved into submission. For his part in break-

*The Chancellor of the Exchequer, his wife, and daughter
Sarah on Budget Day in 1929.*

ing the strike Winston Churchill earned the bitter enmity of British workers.

During the next few years, relations between Prime Minister Baldwin and Churchill became strained. Churchill again assumed the position of the lone dissenter. His extremes of behavior, his un-swerving conviction that he was always right made even the most reactionary Conservatives wary of him. In particular, he had strong feelings on the India question. Unlike Baldwin and the majority of the Conservatives, Churchill opposed dominion status for India. On this issue he dissociated himself from Baldwin and his supporters.

Churchill was nearing his sixtieth birthday. He had fought in numerous wars and had headed al-most every ministry in the government. Several times over he had seen himself the most popular and then the most unpopular man in the country. It looked now as though he had finally dug his own political grave.

"Winston Is Back!"

In 1931 Winston Churchill came to America on a
lecture tour. He traveled with his wife and daughter,
a secretary and Sergeant Walter H. Thompson of
Scotland Yard. Thompson had been assigned to
guard the now internationally famous figure. No
sooner had Churchill landed in New York than he
dashed off alone to see his good friend Bernard
Baruch, the American statesman and financier. This
impulsive visit came to an abrupt end when Churchill stepped off the sidewalk at a busy intersection.
Forgetting that American traffic keeps to the right,
he lunged out into the avenue after a glance to the
right and was knocked unconscious by a taxicab.
Churchill was taken to the hospital with a dislocated
shoulder and numerous painful lacerations. During
his enforced rest in the hospital, he dictated a hu-

morous article about his accident and sold it to an American magazine for $2,500. This tidy sum afforded him a vacation in the Bahamas when his hospitalization was terminated.

When Churchill returned to Chartwell, after his rugged American lecture tour, he gathered around him a staff of secretaries and began to dictate his biography of the first Duke of Marlborough. He himself was inexhaustible, but his secretaries had to work in relays to keep up with him.

A somewhat battered Churchill leaves the hospital after his traffic accident in New York City.

While Churchill was laboring away at this monumental task, Adolf Hitler and his Nazi followers were storming through Germany, terrorizing, burning and killing in their quest for power.

Churchill, in the seclusion of his study, was not so engrossed in ancient history that he wasn't aware of the dangerous fanatic in Germany. He wrote dozens of articles warning that Hitler was secretly rearming Germany and that he would one day try to rule the world. From his seat in Parliament Churchill warned his country again and again to prepare for the Nazi threat.

His warnings went unheeded. The general attitude of both the government and the English people was that Churchill was dramatizing and exaggerating again. Besides, most Britishers recalled too vividly the dark days of World War I.

Fortunately there were some important people in England who understood and agreed with what Churchill was saying. Among them were military men, scientists and diplomats. They, too, did everything in their power to arouse England from its lethargy. Yet even in 1936, when Hitler flagrantly violated the Versailles Treaty by moving his armies into the demilitarized zone of the Rhineland, England slumbered on.

Into this dangerous situation there dropped a bombshell that was temporarily to distract England from world affairs. A royal battle was brewing, and

Churchill naturally found himself in the thick of it. Edward VIII, who had been king for only a few months, announced that he wanted to marry an American woman who had been twice divorced. When the King made known his marriage plans on December 1, 1936, the nation was shocked. Prime Minister Baldwin stated that if Edward VIII insisted upon marrying a divorced woman he would be violating every tradition of the British monarchy.

The King sought out the council of Winston Churchill, whom he had known for years. Churchill, who was deeply sympathetic with his sovereign's predicament, went before the House of Commons. He pleaded for reasonable and calm Parliamentary discussion of the issue at the appropriate time. Unfortunately many House members believed that Churchill's intervention was motivated merely by personal ambition. As a result, his speech was received with fierce resentment.

On December 10th Edward VIII abdicated his throne, and was given the title of Duke of Windsor. His brother became King George VI.

After King George VI was crowned, Prime Minister Baldwin retired. At his suggestion, King George appointed Neville Chamberlain, a member of a distinguished political family, to replace him. Chamberlain admired Churchill personally, but disagreed with his views on Hitler. Thus Churchill was not included in the Chamberlain Cabinet.

The new Prime Minister wanted peace at any cost. Unlike Churchill, he firmly believed that a policy of appeasement would pacify Hitler. Even after the Germans marched into Austria, Hitler's intentions were not recognized by Chamberlain.

Neville Chamberlain's predicament during the crucial months before the outbreak of World War II was aptly put by Churchill:

> His all-pervading hope was to go down in history as the Great Peacemaker; and for this he was prepared to strive continually in the teeth of facts, and face great risks for himself and his country. Unhappily, he ran into tides the force of which he could not measure, and met hurricanes from which he did not flinch, but with which he could not cope . . . .

Chamberlain could not cope with Adolf Hitler's insatiable appetite for land.

After the annexation of Austria into the Third Reich, Hitler turned his attention to the Sudeten part of Czechoslovakia, which contained a large German population. The Sudetenland, he reasoned, could be another bloodless conquest. He doubted very strongly that Britain and France would go to war over this territory on the behalf of the Czechs. Adolf Hitler was correct.

During a meeting at Munich on the night of September 29, 1938, Chamberlain and Premier Edouard Daladier of France acceded to Hitler's demands.

*Neville Chamberlain (left) and Adolf Hitler at their first
meeting to discuss the fate of Czechoslovakia.*

Shortly after, the first wave of German troops
marched without interference into the Sudetenland.
Czechoslovakia had no alternative but to comply.
The little democratic country had been warned pre-
viously that she could not depend upon the aid of
her allies if she offered any resistance.

In all fairness to Chamberlain it must be said
that he sincerely felt the Sudetenland annexation
was best for the welfare of the Czechs. By acceding
to Hitler's demands, he had avoided unnecessary
bloodshed.

The people of England cheered the Munich Agreement. Britain was not prepared for war, and an intense longing for peace dominated the country. Winston Churchill, however, saw the dangers of the Munich Agreement and rose in a towering rage to address Parliament. "It is necessary," he thundered, "that the nation should realize the magnitude of the disaster into which we are being led. The partition of Czechoslovakia under Anglo-French pressure amounts to a complete surrender by the Western democracies to the Nazi threat of force."

It was not until March 10, 1939, that Hitler's true intentions were realized by Chamberlain and the English people. On that date Hitler announced the incorporation of the remainder of Czechoslovakia into the Third Reich. Too late Chamberlain realized that Hitler's promises for peace were worthless.

It seemed likely to Chamberlain that Poland would be the next victim of Nazi aggression. As a result, he declared that Great Britain would go to war if Poland's independence was threatened. Hitler accepted the challenge.

On September 1, 1939, German tanks rolled into Poland. That same day Chamberlain sent Hitler an ultimatum to withdraw from Poland. Hitler ignored it.

Further British warnings received the same fate.

On September 3, 1939, Neville Chamberlain finally declared that a state of war existed between Great

Nazi troops beginning to move toward the Polish border on August 28th.

Britain and Germany. On this same day he offered Winston Churchill the position of First Lord of the Admiralty. Churchill promptly accepted and just as promptly set to work to bring himself up to date on the fleet and its movements. One of England's greatest sea lords was again at the helm, and the message was flashed to the whole fleet: "Winston is back!"

PART THREE

THE FINEST HOUR

*"War is very cruel. It goes
on for so long."*

The War Leader

The first few months of World War II went badly for the Allies. Hitler's soldiers swallowed up Denmark overnight, then invaded German-infiltrated Norway, where they met only ineffectual opposition from the Allies. The French, whose survival depended on maintaining their famed defense system known as the Maginot Line, complained that Britain was not sending over enough troops.

Meanwhile, on August 23, 1939—just before the outbreak of war—Russia had made a nonaggression pact with Hitler. She then proceeded to move her frontiers westward into eastern Poland and the Baltic countries. The situation on the European continent was indeed bleak for the Allies. Yet Neville Chamberlain felt that the war was going well.

In the spring of 1940 an intensely dissatisfied

Parliament met to get an accounting from the Prime
Minister. Why had England steadily retreated from
Hitler's relentless march through Europe? The
country was now aroused to fury at the ease with
which the Nazi dictator had taken Norway. After
three years of Chamberlain's leadership, even some
members of his own party realized that their Prime
Minister was not the man to lead his country to
victory. The debate in Parliament, which began on
May 7th and lasted for several days, turned into a
bitter attack on Neville Chamberlain, who stubbornly continued to fight for his political life.

On May 9th the House voted on the Chamberlain government's conduct of the war. The results
of the voting showed a definite lack of confidence
in the Prime Minister. Even though he won by a
small majority, more than thirty Conservatives
voted with the Opposition. Soon afterward, Neville
Chamberlain resigned.

On the evening of May 10th, King George VI
sent for Churchill and asked him to form a coalition government. This was the moment for which
Churchill had been waiting, the climax of a stormy
lifetime spent on real and political battlefields. When
he was sworn into office, Churchill was over sixty-
five years old. At an age when most men retire to the
leisure and comfort of home, Churchill was about
to open the most challenging chapter in the history
of England.

In his first address to the House as Prime Minister, Churchill struck that note of grandeur and hope which was to inspire and sustain the British people throughout the war. "I have nothing to offer but blood, toil, tears, and sweat. . . . Come then, let us go forward together with our united strength." Skeptical at first of Churchill's appointment, the grim, worried House rose and drowned out the rest of his words with cheers.

Churchill's first month as Prime Minister was a discouraging one. The Nazis, in their concentrated drive toward the Channel ports, captured Holland on May 15th. On the same day Churchill received a telephone call from Premier Reynaud of France. Reynaud was hysterical with the dreadful news he had to convey. "We are defeated!" he cried over and over again to the stunned Churchill. The Prime Minister learned that German troops, in a new offensive, had broken through a section of the French front line. Within a matter of hours Churchill was conferring with French war leaders in Paris. He managed to convince the French not to surrender, but he was shocked to discover how many weaknesses existed in the highly rated Maginot Line defenses. Less than two weeks after this meeting in France, Churchill received word that Belgium had surrendered.

The Belgian surrender left the Allies in a desperate position. The entire British Expeditionary

Force, in addition to large numbers of French, Polish and Belgian troops, was now utterly trapped by the German forces. The only possible course was for the troops to retreat to Dunkirk, a city in the north of France, and then attempt to return to Britain by way of the English Channel.

The Admiralty broadcast an appeal to the nation. Anything that would float—from rowboat to luxury yacht—was needed at once to help bring back the men from Dunkirk. Such a flotilla as set out to rescue the British Army has never been seen before or since. About 850 vessels eventually took part in the operation.

The evacuation began on the night of May 26, 1940, and continued for nine days under savage and continuous dive-bombing attacks. In the end, more than 300,000 soldiers were successfully evacuated to England. But unfortunately for the Allies precious equipment had to be left behind on the beaches.

The Dunkirk evacuation was a tremendous moral victory for the English people. As Churchill himself wrote in *Their Finest Hour:*

> In the midst of our defeat glory came to the island people, united and unconquerable; and the tale of the Dunkirk beaches will shine in whatever records are preserved of our affairs.

Less than a month after the Dunkirk evacuation, France capitulated to Germany at Compiègne, the

British soldiers form a human chain to wade to a rescue ship off the shore of Dunkirk.

identical site of the German armistice at the end
of World War I. Great Britain now stood alone.

Despite the collapse of France after six weeks of
war, England was determined to fight on. Churchill
expressed the emotion of the whole country when
he said:

> Let us therefore brace ourselves to our duties and
> so bear ourselves that, if the British Empire and its
> Commonwealth last for a thousand years, men still will
> say, "This was their finest hour."

Churchill unified the English people and gave
them confidence in themselves. Their spirit of resistance strengthened, the whole country went to
work to increase aircraft production, build defenses
and establish a Home Guard.

While England worked feverishly to produce guns,
shells and planes, Hitler was massing an invasion
army just across the Channel. He boasted that England would soon be wiped out. The quick capitula-
tion of France, however, had caught Hitler unprepared for a full-scale invasion of England. The British
had an uneasy respite in which to rearm for the assault they knew was coming. Churchill drove himself and his ministers without mercy. Nothing and
nobody was to be spared in the life-and-death struggle that was looming.

In the summer of 1940 the German Luftwaffe began

to send swarms of bombers over England. The German plan was first to wipe out the southern English ports and the Royal Air Force and its airfields, and then to proceed with the invasion. Eventually London became a principal target of the German Luftwaffe. Hitler felt that if he could destroy the capital of the British empire, he would surely bring England to her knees. But as the months rolled by, the German fliers began to meet stiff resistance. Young British pilots went up in their Spitfires and Hurricanes and shot hundreds of German bombers out of the skies.

This was the start of the Battle of Britain—Hitler's first major defeat. The Royal Air Force fought back so fiercely that Hitler eventually had to abandon his daylight attacks.

Driven out of the skies by day, the Luftwaffe resumed the blitz at night. Almost every night for two months London was a city in flames. Every morning the weary, war-torn city shook off the rubble and debris, put out the hundreds of fires still burning, and then prepared itself grimly for nightfall. The nights seemed endless as the screaming bombs and roaring anti-aircraft guns clashed in mortal combat. Thousands of Londoners slept in the subways during the nightly bombardment. In the mornings they went to work in munitions and aircraft factories more determined than ever to keep the Nazis from setting foot on English soil.

Almost every night for two months London was a city in flames.

The air attacks fanned out to other cities and towns throughout England. But the people took the punishment and held firm.

At the close of 1940 a severely battered England was proudly holding her own in the struggle. It seemed incredible—except to the British themselves.

The Prime Minister tours a bombed-out city to offer comfort and courage to his people.

Londoners saw a great deal of the Prime Minister in those agonizing days. The man who had once been hated by the working people was now their beloved "Winnie." He was their leader in a great and terrible war, yet he found time to go out into the streets to talk with them and give them courage to fight on.

It was during the London blitz that Churchill designed another unique outfit for himself. It was something like a baby's zip-up snowsuit, pale-blue in color. He assured his puzzled colleagues that it saved precious minutes of getting into regular clothes and shoes when the sirens screamed their warning and he wanted to dash out to see the "fun." He called it his "siren suit."

Churchill's bodyguard, now promoted to Inspector Thompson, had one of the most difficult jobs in England. Air-raid sirens to Churchill were an irresistible summons to go out into the street, and on occasion Inspector Thompson had to use physical force to keep his charge from being killed by a bomb.

Once during a blitz Churchill stood outside his official residence, 10 Downing Street. Thompson, standing beside the Prime Minister, heard the piercing whistle of a bomb falling quite close. He grabbed the Prime Minister and flung him inside the house. The bomb exploded in the street. For his trouble, Thompson received a sharp scolding from Churchill.

Thompson and other members of Churchill's staff

coped not only with their employer's high spirits but with his exacting standards, impatience and outbursts of temper as well. The British statesman was a hard taskmaster and expected the impossible from all.

He usually spent week ends at Chequers, the official country residence of British prime ministers. His guests were always high-ranking officials, who came away exhausted from a "relaxing" week end in the country. Churchill held meetings, discussed strategy, gave instructions and threw out bold new ideas on how to win the war. When his tireless energies drooped, he enjoyed watching movies, particularly American movies. If he liked a certain picture he would show it over and over again.

Hitler's next major blow fell in a totally unexpected direction. On June 22, 1941, the German army struck like lightning at Russia and, like lightning, left total destruction in its path. At first many Russians, dissatisfied with their government, looked upon the Germans as liberators. Then, when the Nazi troops began killing off large numbers of inhabitants for no apparent reason, the Russians began to resist fiercely.

Although a staunch opponent of communism, Churchill, within hours after the German attack, announced in a radio speech that Britain would give Russia all possible assistance. "The Russian danger," he said, "is our danger . . . ."

The German invasion of Russia gave England a short reprieve. Hitler pulled his planes out of the English skies, mobilized his far-flung armies and threw his whole military might into a smashing assault on Russia. But Hitler, who was in some ways a genius, had forgotten one thing—the Russian winter is the mortal foe of any would-be conqueror.

Since the beginning of the war, Churchill had been in regular correspondence with America's president, Franklin D. Roosevelt. Roosevelt was a warm admirer of England, and he was enormously impressed with the courage and leadership shown by Churchill. Largely through Roosevelt's efforts the United States Congress passed the Lend-Lease measure, which provided Great Britain and her allies with much-needed American guns, tanks, ammunition and planes. America was fast realizing that the greedy Hitler would not stand still even if he devoured all of Europe.

In August of 1941, a secret meeting was held between Churchill and Roosevelt off the coast of Newfoundland. It was a daring undertaking, considering that German U-boats infested the North Atlantic waters. The American and British ships reached the rendezvous point safely, and the moment of meeting was charged with emotion. The personalities of Roosevelt and Churchill acted like magnets

The warm friendship of President Roosevelt and Winston Churchill began during the Atlantic Charter meeting on the high seas.

one upon the other. They were immediately drawn together by a bond of friendship and mutual admiration which lasted until the death of President Roosevelt.

During this conference, the American president asked Inspector Thompson how well the Prime Minister was holding up under the strain of his pressing duties. Thompson gave a favorable report, saying that Churchill had magnificent reserves of strength, slept beautifully and practiced fine work habits. At the end of the conversation, as recorded in Thompson's book, *Assignment: Churchill*, Roosevelt said:

"Well, take care of him. He's about the greatest man in the world. In fact he may very likely *be* the greatest. You have a terrible responsibility in safeguarding him. You have the responsibility of four or five hundred million people, Thompson."

The outcome of the historic meeting between Churchill and Roosevelt was the Atlantic Charter, which ultimately served as the basis for the United Nations organization. The United States, still a neutral nation, committed herself to give all possible aid to the freedom-loving nations enslaved by Nazi Germany.

Four months later, on December 7, 1941, the Japanese bombed the great American naval base at Pearl Harbor. Most of America's fleet in the Pacific was wiped out by the sneak attack. The United States, infuriated by this piece of treachery, rallied at once to the President's request for a declaration of war.

In the early days after America's entry into the war it seemed as though the British Empire would be wiped out before the United States could sufficiently mobilize its industry and man power for the great struggle ahead. Shortly after the Pearl Harbor attack, two of England's greatest vessels, the *Prince of Wales* and the *Repulse*, were sunk by bombs and torpedoes from attacking Japanese planes. These two crushing naval defeats left the British and Americans in a dreadful position. Encountering only feeble opposition, the Japanese swooped southward and gobbled up Malaya, Burma and Singapore.

The situation in Africa was bad, too. The Germans and Italians, under General Erwin Rommel, had driven the British Army back across the Libyan desert to the Egyptian border.

Miraculously England survived even these deadly blows. Tanks, guns and airplanes were moved as quickly as possible from great American industrial centers to convoys for delivery to England. But the United States was still seriously unprepared for a global war. She had to equip her own troops and build ships to transport them to the Pacific, Europe and North Africa. At the same time the demands made on her by her allies were enormous. Britain and Russia were clamoring for badly needed supplies. It would take from at least six months to a year to organize such a vast operation.

By the middle of December, 1941, Churchill decided it was time to go to America for personal talks with President Roosevelt. He was worried that America would concentrate on the war in the Pacific, and he hoped that his presence in the United

States would keep America's attention focused on beating the Germans.

The strain on the sixty-seven-year-old Prime Minister was beginning to show. For the past two years he had worked at a frenzied pace, directing his armed services in the far-flung theaters of war. He had even flown to North Africa several times to discuss tactics with his generals there. President Roosevelt and Churchill's own doctor were worried about him and urged him to take a brief rest in the Florida sun. Churchill must have been truly exhausted for he accepted the suggestion without arguing. After a few days of relaxation in Florida he left for Bermuda, where the battleship *Duke of York* was waiting to take him back to England.

During his flight to Bermuda in a Boeing flying boat, Churchill made friends with the pilot and even took over the controls awhile. Confident of the plane's efficiency, he asked the pilot if it could make the thirty-five-hundred-mile journey from Bermuda to England. The pilot assured the Prime Minister that such a trip could be made.

The other members of Churchill's party were skeptical at first. Although flights across the Atlantic Ocean were not uncommon at that time, there was not much transatlantic flying in the winter. Wouldn't it be safer, they asked, to make the trip home by boat as planned? However, with typical Churchillian logic, the Prime Minister convinced them that flying would be just as safe as traveling on a battleship exposed to torpedoes.

The Boeing flying boat was refueled at Bermuda, and the next day at 2:00 P.M. set out on one of the strangest adventures of the war. Everything was fine for the first few hours. Then the plane ran into bad weather. For hours the pilot flew in dense mist and compulsory radio silence. Shortly before they were due to arrive in England, the pilot informed his passengers that he could not determine their exact location. Luckily a member of Churchill's party was able to determine the correct course, and the plane eventually landed safely at an English airport.

Upon landing Churchill learned that, had the Boeing continued on its incorrect course, it would have flown over German-occupied Brest. To make the situation even more frightening, the plane had been picked up on British radar screens and designated as an enemy bomber coming in from Brest. Six Hurricanes had been dispatched to shoot it down. Fortunately for Churchill and his party the Hurricanes had not been able to locate the Boeing.

Churchill afterward cabled President Roosevelt to tell him that it had been a smooth flight with a tail wind all the way.

The Tide Turns

During the months that Britain stood alone, Churchill's official title was Prime Minister, but in practice he also directed the Army, Navy and Royal Air Force. He worked eighteen hours a day and, as had always been his custom, he allowed his interests and activities to spill over into departments that were not at all his concern. Throughout the first eighteen months of his leadership, the full support of the country was behind him, although he was not entirely exempt from criticism.

Toward the end of 1941 Churchill began to receive heavy criticism from the press, various pressure groups and some factions of Parliament for his conduct of the war. After a year and a half of super-human effort—in the factories at home, on the battle-fields and at sea—Britain had nothing but staggering losses to show for her tremendous endeavor. Naturally someone had to take the blame. The press began to wonder in print if the Prime Minister wasn't getting a bit too old to direct the policy of all the war ministries himself. There were rumblings in Parliament that perhaps Churchill had better step down in favor of a younger man. Wouldn't it be better for the war effort, other outspoken critics were saying, if Churchill just confined himself to the political side of the war and appointed a minister of defense to relieve him of that stupendous burden?

Shortly after his return from the United States, Churchill decided to go before Parliament for a vote of confidence. Masses of accumulated work awaited his attention, but he had made up his mind to hold a debate on the course of the war. All criticism could then come out in the open, and he would have an opportunity to defend himself.

A great deal depended on the speech Churchill was going to make in Parliament. He had to convince his critics that his had been the right procedure, despite the terrible failures. Far more difficult was the news that he had to break: The situation would get much worse before it began to improve. But improve it would, and he was certain of victory in the Far East, the Mediterranean and the African desert.

While he was preparing his speech, Churchill asked Field-Marshal Alanbrooke to drop by. Alanbrooke found the Prime Minister propped up in bed, dressed in a red and gold oriental dressing-gown. His bed was littered with papers and dispatches, and the customary cigar was sticking out of his mouth. The bell was continually being rung for secretaries, typists or Churchill's faithful valet, Sawyers. Alanbrooke wrote in his diary:

> The red and gold dragon dressing-gown in itself was worth going miles to see, and only Winston could have thought of wearing it. He looked rather like some Chinese mandarin. . . .

During his speech before Parliament, Churchill said:

> I am the man that Parliament and the nation have got to blame . . . and I cannot serve them effectively unless, in spite of all that has gone wrong, and that is going wrong, I have their trust and faithful aid.

This was a new Churchill, a humble man, asking his countrymen not to lose faith in him. At the end of the debate, a vote of 464 to 1 reaffirmed the confidence of Parliament in its Prime Minister.

As Churchill had warned, things did get much worse for the Allies before they began to improve. The first six months of 1942 were grim. In addition to further setbacks in the Pacific and North Africa, Allied losses at the hands of German U-boats con-

tinued to be appalling. On the eastern front Russia
was still engaged in a life-and-death struggle with
German troops.

In June Churchill flew to Washington for another
conference with President Roosevelt. American and
British scientists were jointly engaged in developing
a powerful new explosive, and Churchill wished to
discuss the progress of the project with Roosevelt.
The new explosive was the atomic bomb.

During this visit, Churchill received what he
considered to be one of the heaviest blows of the
war. On June 21st, he learned that Tobruk in North
Africa had been seized by General Rommel's army.
As a result, more than 30,000 British soldiers had
been taken prisoner. The defeat was a calamity since
most of Britain's efforts in the war had been put
into the North African campaign.

Again the government's conduct of the war was
questioned. This time Churchill did not have to
request a vote of confidence. A motion of censure
against the government was introduced in the House.

For several days the members of the House engaged in a heated discussion of the censure motion.
Since Churchill's Cabinet was extremely loyal, as
was most of the House, the motion of censure was
defeated by a vote of 475 to 25.

After Russia entered the war on June 22, 1941,
Premier Joseph Stalin kept insisting that Eng-

land open a second front. After the United States
joined the fighting, his demands for a second front
in North Africa or in France became more and more
persistent. A second front would divert many Nazi
divisions from the massive concentration in Russia.

It was difficult to convince Stalin that England
and the United States were not yet prepared for
such a step, much as they would like to undertake
it. There simply were not enough available troop
ships, landing craft and planes to cover a massive
invasion.

Churchill, beset by the demands of Russia for a
second front and shocked by the discouraging defeats in the North African campaign, made a typi-
cally Churchillian decision. He would fly to Cairo
and see for himself what was wrong with his desert
command. Then, after studying the situation in
Egypt, he would fly to Moscow and explain to Stalin
why it was impossible at the moment to open a second front in France.

His doctor pleaded with him not to risk such a
hazardous trip. The strain on his health would be
enormous. Members of his Cabinet were also worried
about the dangers of flying over the Mediterranean.
But Churchill was never one to be frightened by
dangers of any kind. He went ahead with his plans,
flying from London to Cairo in a Liberator bomber.

In Cairo he reached his own conclusions about
the series of British defeats, and then made a series

General Harold Alexander (left) and General Bernard Montgomery, two important figures in the North African campaign.

of decisions which greatly strengthened the British position in North Africa. First he divided the North African military command into two separate divisions—the Near East and the Middle East. Next he appointed General Harold Alexander as the new

commander of the British Middle East forces, while
he put the British Eighth Army command into the
hands of General Bernard L. Montgomery. His instructions were that General Rommel must be
beaten. Then Churchill flew off to Moscow for his
first meeting with Stalin.

Stalin and Churchill had many qualities in com-
mon. They were both ardent patriots, and each was
ready to die for his country. Both men, although
politically worlds apart, had a profound grasp of
political and military affairs. And both had a capa-
city for food and drink that stunned their respective
staffs.

The first few meetings between Stalin and Churchill were charged with tension. Stalin was frequently
rude and insulting. He baited Churchill, accusing
the British of not really fighting the war at all.
Churchill was infuriated by these unfair charges.
Not a bit intimidated by the Russian dictator, he
pounded on the table and angrily told the Russians
a few hard facts about what Great Britain had been
doing. Stalin, a fighter like Churchill, did not take
offense. Instead, he said something to the effect that
he admired Churchill's fighting spirit.

During the conferences which took place in August
of 1942, Churchill, by agreement with President
Roosevelt, explained to Stalin why there could be
no invasion of France that year. However, the United
States and England had agreed there was another

way to divert large forces of Germans. A large-scale
North African offensive called "Operation Torch"
was being planned. As soon as the men and supplies
necessary for such an operation were assembled,
the invasion would be launched by the Allies. Despite
some uncomfortable moments during the talks,
Churchill managed to convince Stalin of the merits
of the North African second front.

On October 23, 1942, General Montgomery threw
his Eighth Army against Rommel's forces at El
Alamein. One thousand British guns opened fire on
the German positions. The battle at El Alamein
turned out to be the first decisive British victory
in the war. The British took about 20,000 prisoners
and captured a great deal of valuable equipment.
The battle of El Alamein was a turning point for the
British. As Churchill wrote, "Before Alamein we
never had a victory. After Alamein we never had a
defeat."

Less than a month later, thousands of British
and American troops landed on the North African
coast. Operation Torch was under way. Months of
desert warfare followed. Then, on May 13, 1943,
General Alexander notified Churchill that all enemy
resistance at Tunis had ended. As a result of this
victory, the Allies were now "masters of the North
African shores."

The North African invasion was a brilliant ex-

ample of organization and cooperation. It was also
the start of the offensive which carried the Allies
forward to ultimate victory.

For the next two years of terrible warfare the
Allies were engaged in continuous aggressive actions.
The leaders of the three great powers—Churchill,
Roosevelt and Stalin—met from time to time at
Casablanca, at Teheran and at Cairo. After June 6,
1944—D-Day, when American, British and Canadian
troops landed in France—the Allies were fairly certain that victory was in their grasp. Peace terms
had to be discussed and prepared. Unconditional
surrender on the part of Germany and Japan would
be the minimum basis for entering into any peace
talks with the enemy.

It was during the Teheran meeting, on November
30, 1943, that Churchill celebrated his sixty-ninth
birthday. He was the host at a large dinner party
which was made very festive with a huge birthday
cake decorated with sixty-nine candles. Even the
usually taciturn Stalin, whose respect and admiration for Churchill had increased with each of their
meetings, was deeply moved on this occasion. Lifting
his glass in a birthday toast, Stalin cried, "To my
fighting friend!"

President Roosevelt presented Churchill with a
porcelain vase. On the birthday card the President
had written: "For Winston Spencer Churchill, on
his 69th birthday at Teheran, Iran, November 30,

Churchill models a Persian lamb hat, a birthday present from British reporters who covered the Teheran meetings.

1943, with my affection and may we be together for many years."

The terrible burdens of war prevented this wish of the President's from coming to pass. At midnight on April 12, 1945, Churchill was notified of President Roosevelt's death. Inspector Thompson, Churchill's faithful bodyguard, found the British Prime Minister in his study, weeping. "I have lost a great friend," Churchill said. "One of the greatest ever . . . ."

The Battles Are Over

Out of the close collaboration of Churchill and Roosevelt during World War II had come plans for the formation of the United Nations. The groundwork for some type of a world organization had been laid early in 1941, when representatives of nine European governments-in-exile joined with Great Britain and the Commonwealth in signing the Inter-Allied Declaration. By signing this document each nation agreed to cooperate with other countries to bring about lasting peace throughout the world. Soon after, Churchill and Roosevelt drafted and then signed the Atlantic Charter while aboard a cruiser off Newfoundland.

During Churchill's visit to the United States in December, 1941, the Prime Minister and President Roosevelt drafted a short document which reaffirmed many of the ideas expressed in the Atlantic Charter. It eventually became known as the Declaration by the United Nations, and in time was signed by forty-seven nations.

Numerous conferences between the Allies were held in the years following the signing of the Declaration by the United Nations. Then, in June, 1945, representatives of fifty nations signed the United Nations Charter which stipulated that all future diplomatic, political and military disputes among these nations would be settled by the United Nations. Thus the ideal world dreamed of by Churchill and Roosevelt seemed, at last, to have a chance of becoming a reality.

On May 7, 1945, representatives of an utterly defeated Germany signed the terms of unconditional surrender. The following day people all over the free world joyfully celebrated the Allied victory in Europe. In England, however, a political crisis began to brew.

Throughout the war the Conservative and Labor parties had joined in a united front, cooperating superbly. With the defeat of Nazi Germany this period of cooperation came to an end, and party rivalries soon flared up anew. Thus Churchill had no choice but to call a General Election, which was held on July 5, 1945. In accordance with British election practices the ballots were counted three

After years of "blood, toil, tears, and sweat," Churchill celebrates the defeat of Nazi Germany. (*Above*) With a peaceful smile he concludes his triumphant broadcast to the country, while (*left*) from a balcony he flashes his famous "V-for-Victory" sign at a cheering crowd.

weeks later on July 26th.

Churchill woke before dawn on the day of the ballot counting with "a sharp stab of almost physical pain." As he has written in *Triumph and Tragedy:*

> . . . A hitherto subconscious conviction that we were beaten broke forth and dominated my mind. All the pressure of great events, on and against which I had mentally so long maintained my "flying speed," would cease and I should fall. The power to shape the future would be denied me. The knowledge and experience I had gathered, the authority and goodwill I had gained in so many countries, would vanish. . . .

Churchill's premonition turned out to be correct. The Conservative party lost the election by an overwhelming majority. On the twenty-sixth of July, Clement Attlee and the Laborites assumed control.

Why did Churchill lose the election? It is true that personal affection for Churchill was still very strong in England, but the masses of people would no longer have any part of his Conservative party. The people hated the party that had been responsible for Munich; they were tired of rationing, tired of making sacrifices. The Labor party had made many bright promises, and the voters apparently wanted what they had to offer.

Churchill brooded in silence for days. The ingratitude of the nation hurt him deeply. He was seventy years old, and it was expected that now, finally, he would retire to the country to tend his garden and paint pictures. But those who thought so were making the same old foolish mistake in their estimate of Winston Churchill.

It was a great wrench to move from 10 Downing Street and Chequers, but once he was back at Chartwell, his own country home, he began to make plans for the future. He also began to paint again for the first time since the war. Gradually the hurt from his political defeat was eased. He turned out a number of fine pictures, how fine he himself did not realize. But in 1947 he submitted two of his works to the Royal Academy under the signature of "Mr. Winter." Out of hundreds of pictures submitted for a Royal Academy exhibition, very few are considered good enough to hang. "Mr. Winter's" two pictures were among those chosen. Now other important art museums in the world exhibit Churchill's paintings.

Pablo Picasso, the famous artist, once said: "If Churchill were a painter by profession, he'd have no trouble making a living." Churchill even wrote a book on the subject entitled *Painting as a Pastime*.

Painting was not Churchill's only occupation at Chartwell. As leader of the Conservative party, he remained active in British politics. And, as a prominent international statesman, he viewed with increasing alarm the infiltration of communism throughout the world. Casting his eye on eastern Europe, he could obtain little satisfaction in knowing that

Puffing away at his cigar, Churchill paints one of his vivid landscapes.

what he had prophesied during the last few years of World War II had come to pass. Eastern Europe, as he had predicted, was now completely under the thumb of communist Russia.

Throughout the Second World War, Churchill had been forced to ally Great Britain with Russia against a dangerous mutual enemy—Nazi Germany.

Although he abhorred everything the Bolshevik state represented, he had no choice. After the successful Normandy invasion of June, 1944, the tide of war had definitely turned in the favor of the Allies. Germany and the Axis powers were doomed, and attention began to focus on territorial settlements that would follow victory. Stalin's relations with the Allied leaders, particularly Winston Churchill, became more strained.

The first major clash between Stalin and the British Prime Minister occurred over Poland. By the end of July, 1944, Russian armies were approaching German-occupied Warsaw. The Polish underground army, which owed allegiance to the Polish anti-communist government-in-exile situated in London, was waiting for the right moment to revolt. Russia began a vigorous air attack on the city and urged the underground to start an uprising at once. The Warsaw underground forces responded by setting off a general insurrection on August 1st, whereupon Russia promptly halted her ground and air attack. In the meantime Germany sent in additional forces to quell the revolt.

Despite American and British pleas and the urgings of Polish communist leaders in Moscow, Stalin refused to assist the Poles and continue the Russian offensive against Warsaw. He even refused to allow American and British planes to land at Russian air bases near the Polish border so that supplies could be delivered to the struggling Poles.

Churchill wished to take drastic action against Russia, but President Roosevelt was opposed to any move that would impair relations among the Allies. A final appeal was sent to Stalin. Finally, on September 10th, Russia offered the Poles some half-hearted assistance. It came too late.

During the more than sixty days of hand-to-hand fighting in the streets of Warsaw, approximately 15,000 men and women of the 40,000-member Polish underground army were slain. And nearly 200,000 of the total civilian population were also killed. The gain of the Warsaw massacre for Stalin was apparent —thousands of anti-communists were eliminated.

By October of 1944, Russian armies were pressing hard elsewhere in eastern Europe, and Churchill was particularly concerned about the fate of Greece. On the 9th he flew to Moscow for personal talks with Stalin. As a result of these talks, Britain was given a free hand in Greece, and Russia was to determine the course of events in Rumania and Bulgaria for the remainder of the war. Britain and Russia would have equal latitude in Hungary and Yugoslavia.

Churchill's concern over Greece was justified. Before the Moscow talks, Greece had been liberated from German occupation, and its exiled government had returned to Athens. By December, Greece was in the throes of a civil war. The Greek communists had rebelled and attempted to capture the capital. On orders from Winston Churchill, British troops stationed in the country were authorized to squelch the communist uprising. The communist rebels were eventually overpowered, and an armistice was signed on January 11th. Communist guerrillas, however, continued to present a problem in Greece for many years to come.

The British government was sharply criticized, particularly by the American press, for its intervention in Greece. The House of Commons was also disturbed. In his speech before the House, Churchill justified the action of the British government as follows:

> . . . Democracy is not based on violence or terrorism, but on reason, on fair play, on freedom, on respecting the rights of other people. Democracy is . . . [not] to be picked up in the street by a man with a Tommy gun. I trust the people, the mass of the people, in almost any country, but I like to make sure that it is the people and not a gang of bandits who think they can overturn constituted authority.

After his speech, Churchill's government won a vote of confidence by a large majority.

Stalin kept his word and did not interfere with the British action in Greece. But before the war was over, Russia had established puppet governments in both Rumania and Bulgaria.

By January, 1945, Churchill, extremely alarmed

over the eastern European political situation, was convinced that another meeting of the "Big Three" was imperative. Roosevelt and Stalin agreed, and a meeting at Yalta was arranged for the following month. Before conferring with Stalin, however, Churchill and Roosevelt met at Malta for preliminary talks. Throughout these discussions, Churchill emphasized the importance of allowing as little territory as possible to fall under Russian domination during the remainder of the war.

At Yalta the question of Poland dominated the conference of the Big Three. Churchill emphasized the fact that Britain had gone to war on Poland's behalf and was most concerned about her future. He spoke of the importance of holding free elections in Poland as soon as possible and the necessity of on-the-spot Anglo-American inspections to evaluate conditions in the country.

Stalin was rather evasive about these demands and disagreed completely with Churchill about the strength of the communists in Poland. He claimed that the majority of Poles wished a communistic form of government.

The question of Polish boundaries was also hotly debated. Stalin wished to extend drastically the western boundaries of the country, in a move that would displace millions of Germans. Churchill was vehement in his objections to this proposal.

At the end of the Yalta meetings, Churchill was

The Big Three—Churchill, Roosevelt and Stalin—at Yalta.

extremely uneasy about the whole Polish situation; he was even more distrustful of his Russian ally.

In the remaining months of war, as the Nazi armies were forced to retreat to their own boundaries, Churchill's opinions on the conduct of the war began to conflict sharply with those held by leaders in the United States. The British Prime Minister relentlessly advocated the advance of Allied armies as far east in Europe as possible. American civilian and military leaders opposed such extended operations. Troops were urgently needed for the battle raging in the Pacific, and the United States hoped for a time that Russia would declare war on Japan. Thus, despite Churchill's objections, both Prague and Vienna fell into Russian hands.

Upon Roosevelt's death in April, 1945, Harry S. Truman, the American vice-president, assumed the presidency. Shortly afterward, Churchill had a serious disagreement with President Truman. Throughout various conferences during the early stages of the war, Stalin, Roosevelt and Churchill had charted out specific postwar occupation zones for Germany in the event of Allied victory. By 1945 a great deal of the Russian-designated territory was occupied by Anglo-American troops.

Churchill, dismayed by Russia's many broken promises, sent a telegram to Truman on April 19th, emphasizing the urgency of holding fast to this territory. To his keen disappointment Truman firmly rejected the idea and announced that he planned to withdraw American troops from the area when the military situation seemed appropriate. Truman believed that the honor of the United States was at stake. Roosevelt had helped to chart the occupation zones, and Truman believed it was his responsibility to see that the arrangements approved by the late president were carried out.

In the months that followed, Churchill continually renewed his plea, but Truman remained steadfast in his decision. On July 1st he ordered American

President Truman and Churchill in Berlin for the Potsdam Conference.

troops to begin their withdrawal from the Russian-designated territories. Since Great Britain could not hold out alone, she had no alternative but to withdraw her own troops as well. An area four-hundred miles long, containing millions of Czechs and Germans, passed into Russian hands. This land, Churchill felt at the time, might have served as influential bargaining power for Great Britain and the United States at the important Potsdam conference to be held later in July.

The announcement, midway through the Potsdam conference, of Churchill's defeat at the British polls cut short his influence on the fate of postwar Europe. But despite his loss of office he continued to urge the Western democracies to be firm in their dealings with Soviet Russia.

In March of 1946 Churchill was invited to Westminster College in Fulton, Missouri, to accept an honorary degree. During his address he said:

> From Stettin in the Baltic to Trieste in the Adriatic, an Iron Curtain has descended across the Continent. Behind that line lie all the capitals of the ancient states of Central and Eastern Europe: Warsaw, Berlin, Prague, Vienna, Budapest, Belgrade, Bucharest and Sofia. All these famous cities and the populations around them lie in what I must call the Soviet sphere. What is needed is a settlement, and the longer this is delayed, the more difficult it will be, and the greater our danger will become. From what I have seen of our Russian friend and ally during the war, I am convinced that there is nothing they admire so much as strength, and there is nothing for which they have less respect than weakness, especially military weakness.

It was the first time anyone had used the expres-

sion "Iron Curtain." Many people criticized Churchill for being so harsh with Russia in that Westminster
speech, but time proved him to be right again.

Among the tasks that kept Churchill fully occupied at Chartwell was one of such stupendous
proportions that any other man would have been
staggered by it. He began to write his history of
World War II. Gathering and sorting the material
was in itself a herculean labor, and he was assisted
in the task by a staff of experts. Eventually, however, it was Churchill himself who wrote every single
word of the monumental six-volume work, published
over a period of years from 1948 to 1954. Churchill's
The Second World War has been translated into
many languages and will no doubt continue to be a
standard reference source as long as men read about
World War II.

Churchill's preoccupation with his history of
World War II did not prevent him from attending
sessions of Parliament and meeting regularly with
the leaders of the Conservative party. He felt the
time was not far off when the English people would
become dissatisfied with the Labor party, and he
was preparing for it.

His opportunity came in 1951 when the Conservatives came back into power. At the age of
seventy-seven Churchill was once again the Prime
Minister of Great Britain!

After casting his ballot in the 1951 General Election, Churchill is surrounded by well-wishers.

Then in 1953 two outstanding honors were be-
stowed upon him. After many years of refusing every
possible distinction the Crown and the government
could confer, Churchill finally accepted the Order
of the Garter in honor of the Coronation of Queen
Elizabeth II in 1953. He was now Sir Winston. In
that same year he received the Nobel Prize for
Literature.

In 1955, at the age of eighty-one, Churchill decided it was time to step aside in favor of a younger
man. He resigned as Prime Minister. Winston
Churchill had fought his last battles, both military
and political. An outstanding career in Parliament
and on the international scene had finally ended.

Throughout his remarkable career the gallantry,
honor, boundless energies, high spirits and resilience
displayed by Winston Churchill set him apart from
other men. Perhaps, however, his most outstanding
quality was his indomitable courage. During his
life he had the necessary strength to rise above defeat, the integrity to stand alone for the sake of his
convictions, the courage to demand sacrifice and
fortitude from the English people at their most trying time in history.

"Never give in!" he said during a speech at Harrow school on October 29, 1941. "Never give in!
Never, Never, Never, Never—in nothing great or
small, large or petty—never give in except to convictions of honor and good sense."

Epilogue

An Author's Personal
Recollection

As a war correspondent in London during the worst days of the blitz, I saw what one great human being —namely, Winston Churchill—could do to hold together a nation literally on the verge of being annihilated. I heard him speak in Parliament a dozen times, and I saw him in the streets after nights of incessant bombing. The valiant spirit of this man fused the ruined city and the shattered populace into one rocklike symbol of defiance.

Those of us who were war correspondents in London in those days tried again and again to get Churchill to hold a press conference, with no success. The White House custom of holding press conferences does not exist in England. Nevertheless, I did persuade Churchill's Parliamentary Secretary, Brendan Bracken, to let me go along on the Prime

Minister's next trip.

A week after Mr. Bracken made the promise, I received a phone call from 10 Downing Street. It was Brendan Bracken with good news. "The Prime Minister is going to inspect some tank maneuvers in the country tomorrow, and I have arranged for you to go along. I'll pick you up at eight-thirty tomorrow morning."

The next morning, a hot day, he drove me to Paddington Station. The station had been severely hit by bombs, and most of its original vaulted glass roof was gone. The brilliant morning sunlight filtered through the open spaces. Bracken told me that we would be leaving in a special train at nine o'clock for Salisbury Plains. The station was quite deserted except for a dozen or so men standing around casually on the platform where the special train stood.

At four minutes to nine two big black cars rolled up to the station. Eight men and one woman stepped out of the cars. The woman was Mrs. Agnes Hill, one of the Prime Minister's secretaries. Then came one of the great moments of my life. Brendan Bracken introduced me to Winston Churchill.

"Well, let's climb aboard," he said, his face breaking into the famous Churchill grin. "It might be cooler in the train."

The train consisted of a locomotive and two cars. One was a luxurious parlor car, the other a dining car. The train left the station at exactly nine o'clock.

The parlor car was extremely comfortable but quite warm.

"Mrs. Hill," Churchill said, "I am sure you won't mind if we take off our coats?"

"Of course not, sir," she said, smiling at all of us. Then she pointed to a dispatch case. "I have this morning's mail with me. Do you want to go over it now?"

"Mail, mail!" Churchill groaned. "We have a hundred letters to answer every day. Well, let's get to it."

There was a desk set up in the rear of the car. While Mrs. Hill read the mail, Churchill dictated the answers rapidly.

Averell Harriman happened to be in London at the time on a special mission for President Roosevelt. He was a good friend of the Prime Minister's, and he was on the train with us for a very good reason. The tanks Mr. Churchill was going to inspect had come from the United States, and Mr. Harriman wanted to find out what the Prime Minister and his experts thought of them. The two military experts in the party were General Sir Hastings Ismay and Major John Churchill, the Prime Minister's brother. During the trip I sat and talked with Averell Harriman.

At noon Churchill finished his dictating. "Come," he said, "let's have some lunch." He herded us all into the dining car and motioned to Mr. Harriman and me to sit with him. It was a good lunch and, when it was over, the steward passed around a box of Churchill's cigars with his initials on the band. I took one and put it in my pocket.

"Don't you smoke cigars?" he asked.

"No, Mr. Churchill, I don't," I answered, embarrassed that he had caught me.

"Then why did you take one?" he growled.

"I'll tell you why," I said uncomfortably. "My father, who lives in Brooklyn, loves cigars. He is also one of your most ardent admirers in America, Mr. Churchill. So I thought I would send him your cigar."

Churchill beamed with delight. "I am glad to hear I am well-known in Brooklyn," he chuckled. "Give Mrs. Hill your father's address, and we'll see that he gets a box."

Two weeks later my father was amazed and delighted to receive a box of cigars with Winston Churchill's card in it.

Shortly after lunch we reached the Salisbury station. Five thousand uniformed men were standing at attention when we stepped off the train. The general in charge and his staff saluted smartly.

"I suppose your men have been standing here a long time, General," said Churchill. "Let's walk along and say hello to them."

The general could hardly conceal his delight. The rest of us groaned. We had to trail after the Prime

Minister who, apparently unaware of the heat, smiled and chatted with the men as he walked along. We knew they would treasure this moment. Churchill made each man feel that he had come down from London just to see him. Finally the review was over. We climbed into our cars and drove into the country five miles away where the tank maneuvers were to be held.

The tanks put on a good show. Churchill discussed the technical details of the tanks on equal terms with the experts. I was lost in the maze of technicalities, but it was easy to see that the Prime Minister was very satisfied with the tanks.

"The first ones you sent us were used in the Libyan Desert. Those were too thin-skinned," he said. "These are just right." By thin-skinned he meant that the steel plates covering the tanks were not thick enough to give ample protection against enemy fire. Finally, about three o'clock, we climbed back into our cars and headed for the station.

A short distance from the station our cars were stopped. A long table had been set up by the side of the road, and soldiers stood behind it ready to serve tea and sandwiches. The general in charge asked, "Would you stop for some refreshment, Mr. Churchill?" One could see that Churchill was about to refuse. He was probably thinking of himself in the comfortable train with his coat off, enjoying some ice-cold drinks. Then he looked at the perspir-

ing soldiers standing stiffly behind the long table.
He smiled and nodded.

Like a mother hen clucking her baby chicks to
her side, he called to us, "Come on, come on. I can't
disappoint these boys." We all had some tea and
sandwiches. Churchill paused to chat with every
one of the men serving the refreshments. Then, after
he shook hands and said good-by to each one of
them, we went on to the station.

"You put on a good show for us today, General,
a really fine show," the Prime Minister said to the
beaming officer. "Wasn't it a fine show, Averell?"
He turned to Harriman.

"It was indeed," Harriman said earnestly. "I do
hope you'll find those tanks of ours up to standard."

"I know we will," the general answered with a
smile.

"And there are many more coming our way,"
Churchill assured the general. "Isn't that right,
Averell?"

"Many more," Harriman said gravely.

"Time to go. We are leaving at five." Churchill
looked at his watch.

The troops were again lined up in front of the
station, and the military band played "For He's a
Jolly Good Fellow." A few of the soldiers began to
sing it, and then the chorus swelled to a roar and
they were all singing it. Churchill stood there with
his hat off, his whole face alight with pleasure. When

the song came to an end he waved his hat to the troops, and we all climbed back onto the train.

We were hot and tired. Once again Churchill told us to take off our coats. He called for cold drinks and a fresh box of cigars. When he saw that we were all settled comfortably, he said reluctantly, "Oh, well, I must get to work." He went back to the desk with Mrs. Hill and dictated all the way back to London. When he said good-by to me he shook my hand firmly.

"Harriman is coming to dinner tomorrow night. Can you make it?"

"I can make it, sir," I said gravely. Reporters can usually make it when a Prime Minister asks them to dinner.

Ten minutes after I arrived at the Prime Minister's official country home, I was made to feel as though I had known the Churchill family for years. Meeting a great public figure on official occasions is quite a different thing from seeing him at home surrounded by his family. Dining with the Churchill family was an experience I shall always remember.

Before dinner we assembled in the large, high-ceilinged drawing room for cocktails. I was introduced to Mrs. Churchill and their charming daughter Mary. Harry Hopkins, President Roosevelt's confidential assistant, was one of the guests and, of course, the ever-present bodyguard, Inspector Thomp-

son, who was one of the family by now.

Churchill was wearing his siren suit. He used to refer to it laughingly as his rompers. "Most sensible suit I ever had," he said. "Did you know that I designed it myself?" he asked, quite pleased with himself. "You notice I have one extra large breast pocket. That's to hold my cigars."

Suddenly Churchill growled, "Mary, where's Nelson?" Mary did not have to answer. From out of a dark corner of the room stalked a large, angry-looking, black cat.

"Nelson is the bravest cat I ever knew. I once saw him chase a huge dog out of the Admiralty. I decided to adopt him and name him after our great Admiral Horatio Nelson."

"You adopted him?" Mary laughed. "Really, Daddy, you know Nelson adopted you. He's being nice to you tonight because he knows we are having salmon for dinner, and he is hoping you will offer him some."

It was a cozy family dinner, and Churchill scarcely mentioned the war. Our first course was smoked salmon and twice, when Mrs. Churchill was not looking, the Prime Minister sneaked pieces of salmon to Nelson.

Ever since his early school days Churchill's brilliance and wit in conversation had held his contemporaries spellbound. That evening at dinner was no exception and I, like so many others, was en-

Churchill poses in his "siren suit," which he designed himself.

tranced by the beauty of his speech and the scope
of the topics he touched upon. He talked about the
books and poems he had read. He reminisced about
his early days in India when, as a young officer, he
first discovered the pleasures of serious reading. Re-
calling his fondness for Rudyard Kipling's stories
and poems about India, he recited "Danny Dever"
and "Gunga Din" to us. Then he said, "Kipling was
a great singer of songs, but of course there was only
one who will last for all time."

His reference to Shakespeare threw him into an
entirely different mood. Churchill knew most of
Shakespeare's famous speeches by heart, and now
the actor in him took over. He rose from the table
and began to deliver the soliloquy from *Hamlet*. He
walked up and down before us, and his wonderful
voice filled the room, The pudgy, stoop-shouldered
man with the round cherubic face was transformed
into the tragic figure of Hamlet. The sonorous voice
went through the long passage without missing a
word.

The main course of dinner was served.

"It's lamb," Mrs. Churchill said.

Churchill tasted it and frowned. "Lamb!" he
said reproachfully. "It's mutton! Really, Clemmy,
can't you do better than this?"

Handsome Clemmy Churchill looked up and smiled
at him. "Remember, Winston, there is a war on."

The Prime Minister grinned and looked at his

wife fondly. Then, for the first time, he began to discuss the war. He talked of the dark days after Dunkirk.

"That was a bad time," he said. "I knew that the Luftwaffe would soon be coming over. We had a great airplane in the Spitfire, but we had not produced many yet. I appointed Lord Beaverbrook Minister of Aircraft Production and I said, 'Get more Spitfires into the sky, Max,' and Max said, 'If God will give me three months, I'll have Spitfires for you.' Well God gave him three months, but there still were not enough Spitfires in the air. I said, 'Max, we need more Spitfires,' and he said, 'Winston, if God will give me two more months, I'll have them for you.' Well," Churchill continued, "God gave him two more months, and when the Luftwaffe came over we were ready.

"Now we are getting stronger," he went on. "Yes, and that evil man knows it. He knows we will beat him. Even at this moment, when his submarines are sinking our vessels in the North Atlantic, even now, when his planes are bombing this island, he knows he is beaten."

Dinner was finished. Mrs. Churchill and Mary left the room. A butler passed cigars, but this time I did not take one. The smoke from Churchill's cigar made a blue-gray haze over the table. He pointed his cigar at the empty chair where his wife had been sitting.

"Hitler would like to be sitting right there now," he said solemnly. "He would like to be talking to me and asking me if there isn't some way out for him." The Prime Minister puffed on his cigar in silence for a few moments. "But there is no way out for him except total defeat," he added quietly.

"I cannot control my temper when I think of the crimes that man Hitler has committed. When this war has been won by us then something will have to be done about Hitler. His philosophy, his tyranny must be stamped out. If my allies agree, I am in favor of trying him in an international court for the crimes he has committed against humanity— and then shoot him. I am sure he feels the same way about me. Mind you," he chuckled, looking archly over his glasses, "I would not like that, but I cannot say that I would blame him."

He switched suddenly to another topic. "Do you know why I hate the Nazis? I hate them because they frown when they fight. They are grim and sullen. Now, take our magnificent Air Force lads— they grin when they fight. I like a man who grins when he fights. But come on upstairs. Mary will be waiting for us, and she'll scold me if I'm late. We're going to see a movie, *Target for Tonight*, the story of our bomber planes. I have seen it twice, but I want to see it again."

We went to the private projection room, where Mary and Mrs. Churchill were waiting for us. Churchill smoked furiously and was as tense as any movie fan when things looked bad for the R.A.F. bomber planes over Germany. He smiled when the bombs hit their Nazi targets, and he drew a deep breath of relief when the planes returned safely home.

When the film was over we went downstairs, and Inspector Thompson told me that my car was ready to take me back to London. The Prime Minister walked to the door with me. It was a dark night, and cold rain slanted down dismally.

"It's a chilly night," he said solicitously. "But there is a warm blanket in the back of the car. Wrap yourself up in it." He shook my hand and bade me good-by. "I hope you will come and visit us again," he called as I walked toward the car.

I looked back as the car pulled away. Just for the moment, the Prime Minister had forgotten the blackout. He stood there in the huge doorway, and the light from the hall silhouetted him—sturdy, rocklike, immovable. His cigar was stuck in the corner of his mouth at a jaunty angle, and his hands were plunged deep in the pockets of his blue rompers. He waved once and grinned. I, too, admire a man who grins when he fights.

OTHER BOOKS
OF INTEREST

BY WINSTON CHURCHILL:

A Churchill Reader. Edited by Colin R. Coote: Houghton Mifflin Company.

A History of the English-Speaking Peoples. Four volumes: Dodd, Mead & Company.

Lord Randolph Churchill. Two volumes: The Macmillan Company.

Marlborough: His Life and Times. Two volumes: Charles Scribner's Sons.

My Early Life: A Roving Commission. Charles Scribner's Sons. Paperback edition: Charles Scribner's Sons.

The Second World War. Six volumes: Houghton Mifflin Company. Paperback edition: Bantam Books.

With the editors of *Life* magazine: *The Second World War.* Abridged one-volume edition: Golden Press, Inc.

War Speeches (1940–5). Cassell & Company, Ltd.

The World Crisis. Six volumes: Charles Scribner's Sons.

ABOUT WINSTON CHURCHILL AND HIS TIMES:

Broad, Lewis: *Winston Churchill: The Years of Preparation.* Hawthorn Books, Inc.

Bryant, Arthur: *Triumph in the West.* Doubleday & Company, Inc.

Bryant, Arthur: *The Turn of the Tide.* Doubleday & Company, Inc.

Coolidge, Olivia: *Winston Churchill and the Story of Two World Wars.* Houghton Mifflin Company.

Cowles, Virginia: *Winston Churchill: The Era and the Man.* Harper & Brothers. Paperback edition: Grosset & Dunlap, Inc.

Harrity, Richard, and Martin, Ralph G.: *Man of the Century, Churchill.* Duell, Sloan & Pearce, Inc.

Le Vien, Jack, and Lord, John: *Winston Churchill: The Valiant Years.* Bernard Geis Associates.

de Mendelssohn, Peter: *The Age of Churchill.* Alfred A. Knopf.

Moorehead, Alan: *Churchill, A Pictorial Biography.* Viking Press.

Moorehead, Alan: *Gallipoli.* Harper & Bros.

Reynolds, Quentin: *The Battle of Britain.* A World Landmark Book, Random House.

Shirer, William L.: *The Rise and Fall of Adolf Hitler.* A World Landmark Book, Random House.

Thompson, Inspector Walter Henry: *Assignment: Churchill.* Farrar, Straus and Young.

INDEX

ABOUT THE AUTHOR

QUENTIN REYNOLDS, who was a war correspondent in London during World War II, met Winston Churchill during the worst days of the blitz; and his deep admiration for the eminent leader gives this book a special warmth and vitality.

Now the well-known author of more than twenty books, Mr. Reynolds began his career as a sports writer for the New York *World*. He has since worked as a reporter and special Berlin correspondent for the International News Service, and as both associate editor and war correspondent for *Collier's* magazine. He has also contributed numerous articles and short stories to magazines across the country, and has appeared frequently on radio and television.

Mr. Reynolds has written a number of popular Landmark Books, including *The FBI, The Battle of Britain, Custer's Last Stand, The Wright Brothers,* and *The Life of Saint Patrick*. He lives in his native New York City.

This title was originally catalogued by the
Library of Congress as follows:

Reynolds, **Quentin James,** 1902–1965.
    Winston Churchill. New York Random House ₁1963₁
    x, 183 p. illus., ports. 22 cm. (World landmark books, W–56)
    Includes bibliography.

    1. Churchill, Sir Winston Leonard Spencer, 1874–1965—Juvenile
literature.

DA566.9.C5R4   j 92   63—7831

Lib. Ed.: ISBN: 394-90556-3

World Landmark Books